RED TAYLOR SWIFT

EASY GUITAR
WITH NOTES & TAB

ISBN 978-1-4803-2140-3

HAL•LEONARD®
CORPORATION
7777 W. BLUEMOUND RD. P.O. BOX 13819 MILWAUKEE, WI 53213

Visit Hal Leonard Online at
www.halleonard.com

CONTENTS

STRUM AND PICK PATTERNS

This chart contains the suggested strum and pick patterns that are referred to by number at the beginning of each song in this book. The symbols ⊓ and ∨ in the strum patterns refer to down and up strokes, respectively. The letters in the pick patterns indicate which right-hand fingers play which strings.

p = thumb
i = index finger
m = middle finger
a = ring finger

For example; Pick Pattern 2
is played: thumb - index - middle - ring

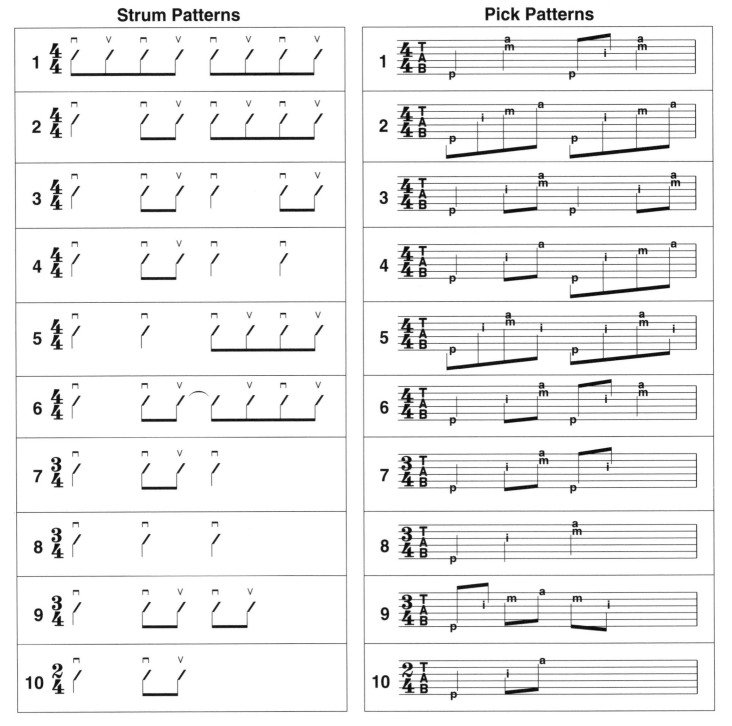

You can use the 3/4 Strum and Pick Patterns in songs written in compound meter (6/8, 9/8, 12/8, etc.). For example, you can accompany a song in 6/8 by playing the 3/4 pattern twice in each measure. The 4/4 Strum and Pick Patterns can be used for songs written in cut time (¢) by doubling the note time values in the patterns. Each pattern would therefore last two measures in cut time.

I Knew You Were Trouble

Words and Music by Taylor Swift, Shellback and Max Martin

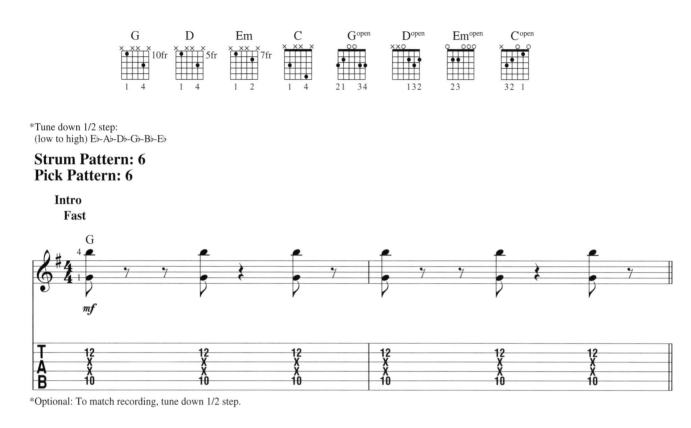

*Tune down 1/2 step:
(low to high) Eb-Ab-Db-Gb-Bb-Eb

Strum Pattern: 6
Pick Pattern: 6

Intro
Fast

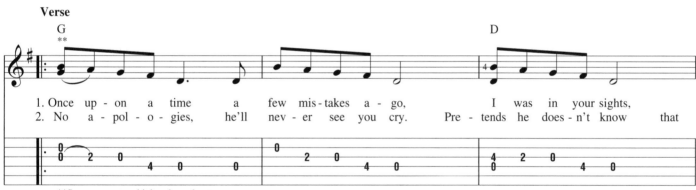

*Optional: To match recording, tune down 1/2 step.

Verse

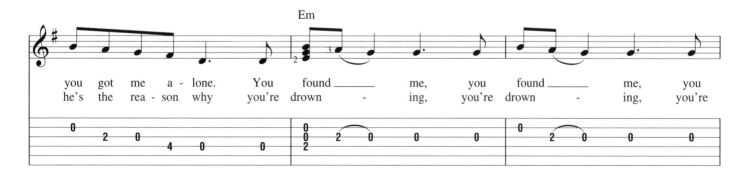

1. Once up-on a time a few mis-takes a-go, I was in your sights,
2. No a-pol-o-gies, he'll nev-er see you cry. Pre-tends he does-n't know that

**Sung one octave higher throughout.

you got me a-lone. You found _____ me, you found _____ me, you
he's the rea-son why you're drown _____ ing, you're drown _____ ing, you're

found _____ me, ee, ee, ee, ee. I guess you did - n't care and I
drown - ing, ing, ing, ing, ing. And I heard you moved _ on from

guess I liked that. And when I fell hard, you took a step back with -
whis - pers on the street. A new notch in your belt is all I'll ev - er be. And

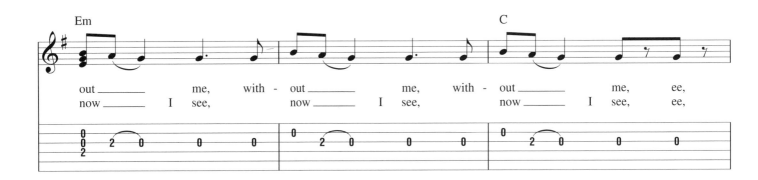

out _____ me, with - out _____ me, with - out _____ me, ee,
now _____ I see, now _____ I see, now _____ I see, ee,

Pre-Chorus

ee, ee, ee. _____ And he's long _____
ee, ee, ee. _____ He was long _____

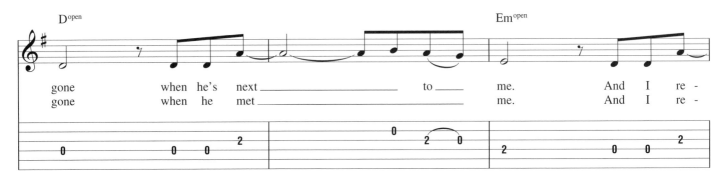

gone when he's next _____ to _____ me. And I re -
gone when he met _____ me. And I re -

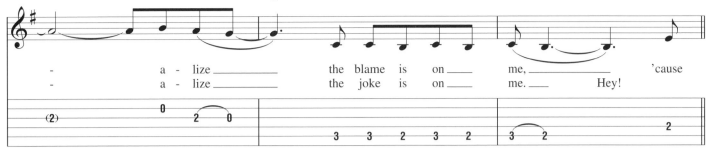

-a -lize _____ the blame is on _____ me, _____ 'cause
-a -lize _____ the joke is on _____ me. ___ Hey!

𝄋 Chorus

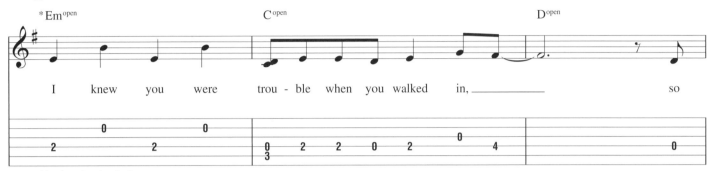

I knew you were trou - ble when you walked in, _____ so

*1st time, let chords ring.
2nd & 3rd times, **Half-time feel**.

shame on me now. _____ Flew me to plac - es I've nev - er been _____

_____ till you put me down. Oh, I knew you were

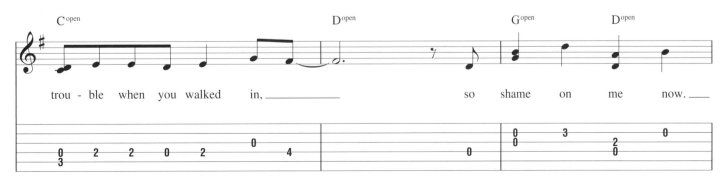

trou - ble when you walked in, _____ so shame on me now. ___

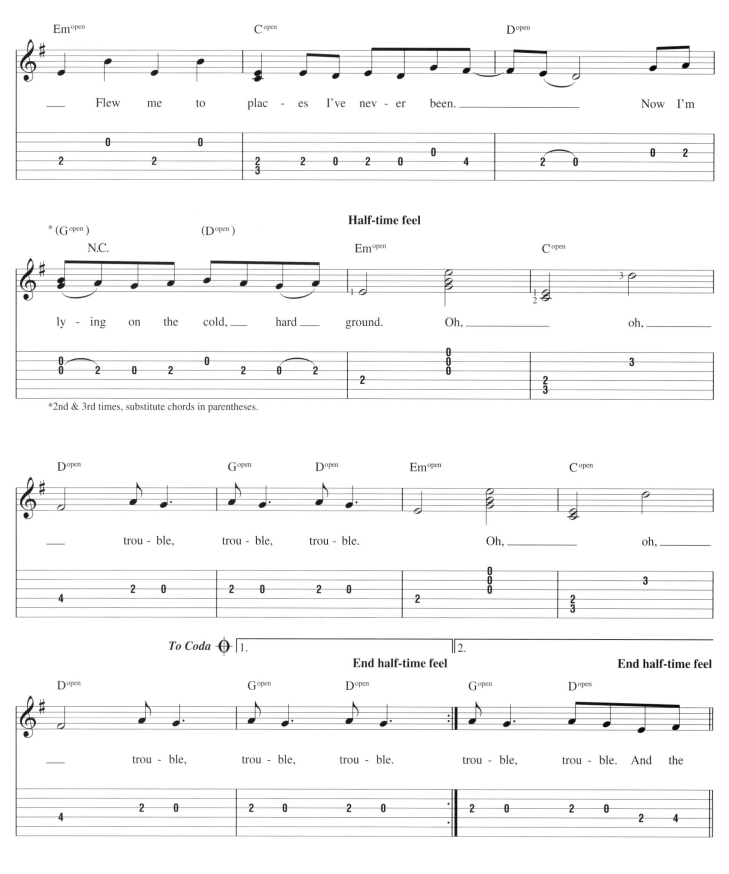

*2nd & 3rd times, substitute chords in parentheses.

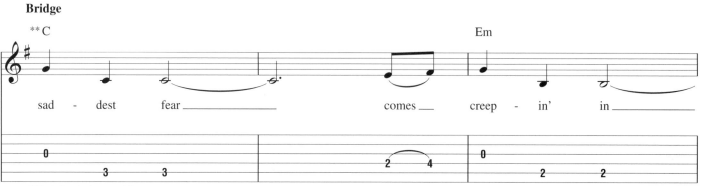

**Let chords ring, next 6 meas.

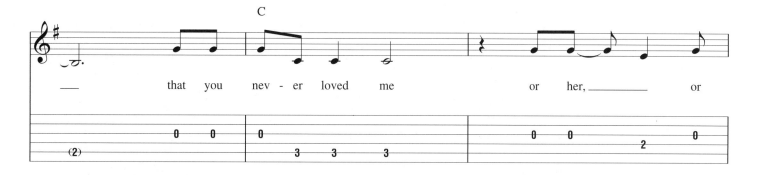

that you nev - er loved me or her, _____ or

D.S. al Coda

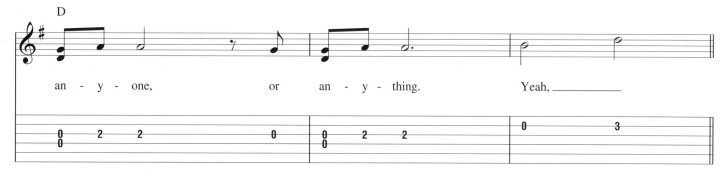

an - y - one, or an - y - thing. Yeah, _____

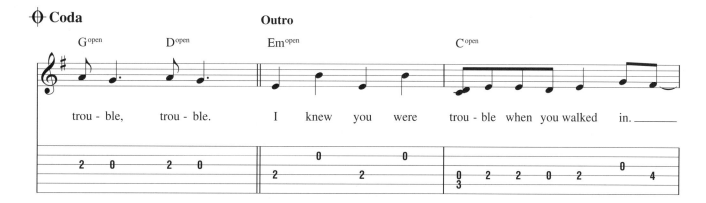

⊕ **Coda**   **Outro**

trou - ble, trou - ble. I knew you were trou - ble when you walked in. _____

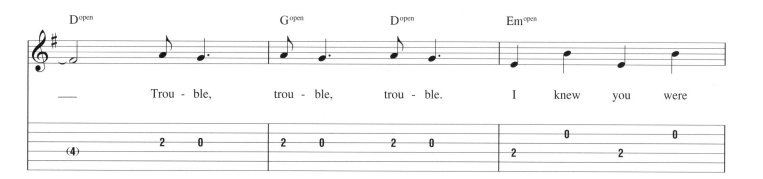

___ Trou - ble, trou - ble, trou - ble. I knew you were

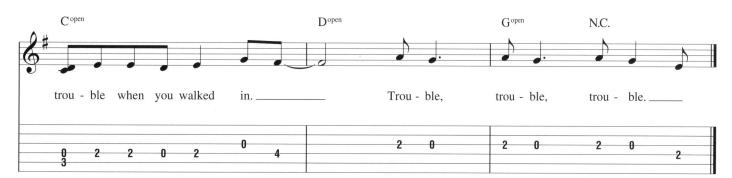

trou - ble when you walked in. _____ Trou - ble, trou - ble, trou - ble. _____

State of Grace

Words and Music by Taylor Swift

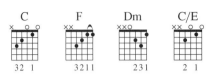

*Capo IV

Strum Pattern: 1
Pick Pattern: 1

Intro
Moderately fast

*Optional: To match recording, place capo at 4th fret.

Verse

1. I'm walk - in' fast ___ through the traf - fic lights, ___ bus - y streets ___ and
We are a - lone ___ with our chang - ing minds. ___ We fall in love ___ till it

bus - y lives ___ and all we ___ know _____ is
hurts or bleeds ___ or fades in time. ___

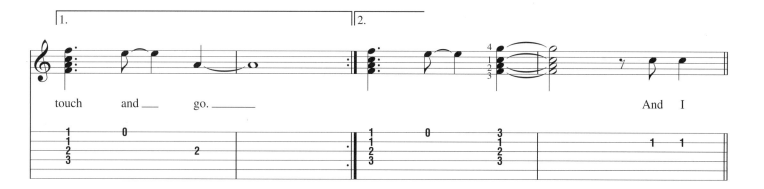

touch and go.

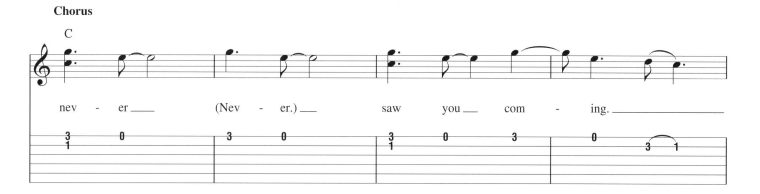

Chorus

nev - er (Nev - er.) saw you com - ing.

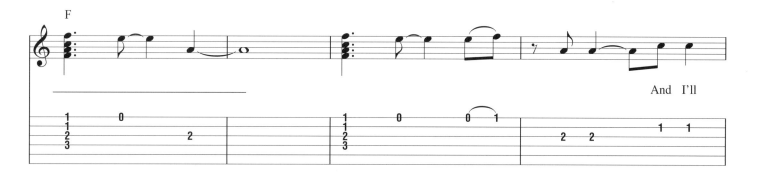

And I'll

nev - er (Nev - er.) be the same.

Interlude

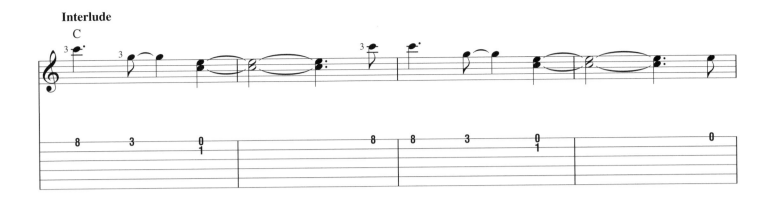

Verse

2. You come a - round __ and the arm - or falls, __ pierce the room __ like a
We are a - lone, __ just a, you and me, __ up in your room __ and our

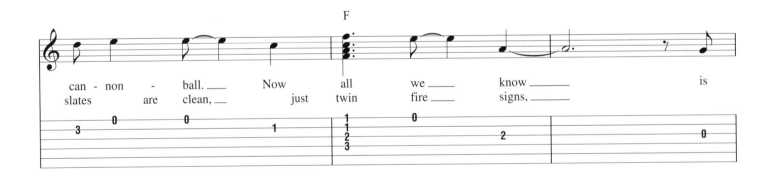

can - non - ball. __ Now all we __ know __ is
slates are clean, __ just twin fire __ signs, __

Pre-Chorus

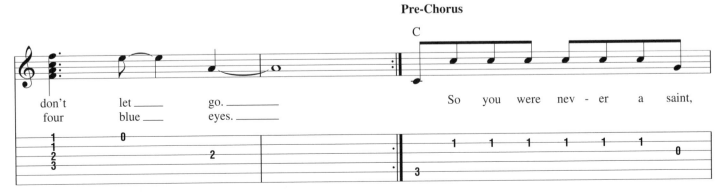

don't let __ go. __ So you were nev - er a saint,
four blue __ eyes. __

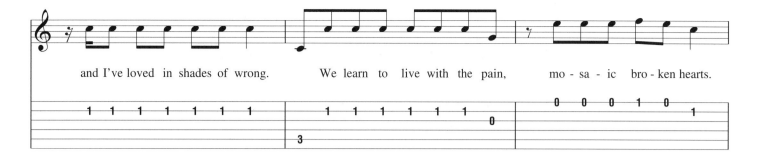

and I've loved in shades of wrong. We learn to live with the pain, mo - sa - ic bro - ken hearts.

But this love is brave and _____ wild. _____ And I

Chorus

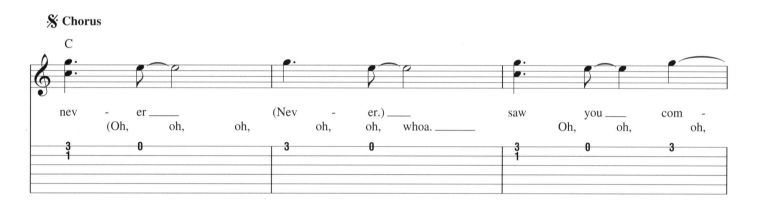

nev - er _____ (Nev - er.) _____ saw you _____ com -
(Oh, oh, oh, oh, oh, whoa. _____ Oh, oh, oh,

- ing. _____
oh, oh, whoa. _____ Oh, oh, oh, oh, oh, whoa. _____ Oh, oh, oh,

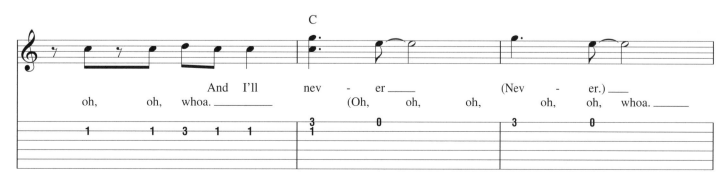

And I'll nev - er _____ (Nev - er.)
oh, oh, whoa. _____ (Oh, oh, oh, oh, oh, whoa. _____

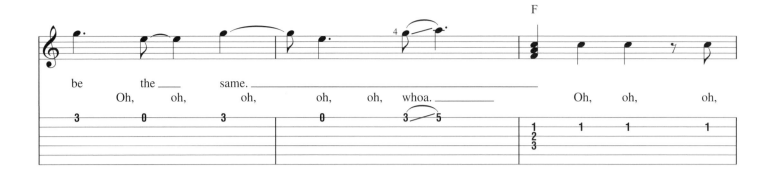

be the ___ same. ___ Oh, oh, oh, oh, oh, whoa. ___ Oh, oh, oh,

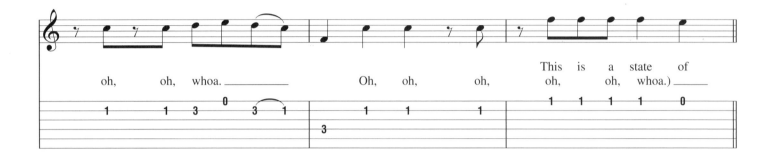

oh, oh, whoa. ___ Oh, oh, oh, oh, oh, whoa.) ___ This is a state of

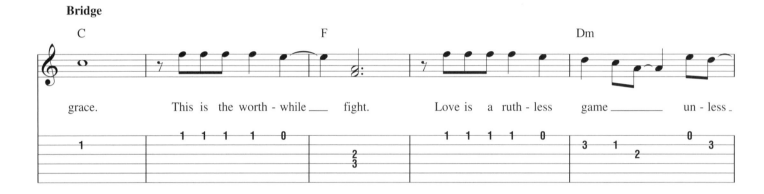

Bridge

grace. This is the worth-while ___ fight. Love is a ruth-less game ___ un-less ___

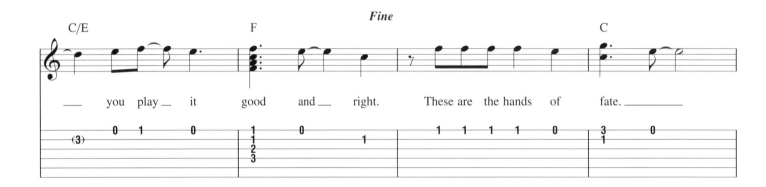

Fine

___ you play ___ it good and ___ right. These are the hands of fate. ___

You're my a-chil-les heel. ___ This is the gold-en age ___ of some - thing

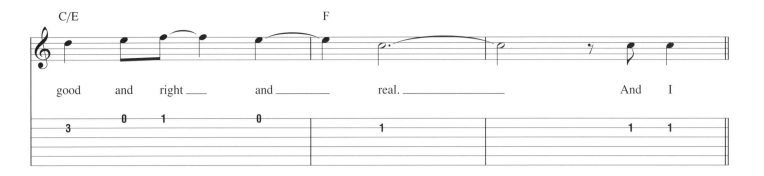

good and right ___ and _____ real. _____ And I

Chorus

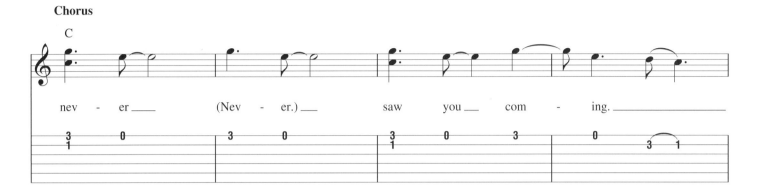

nev - er ___ (Nev - er.) ___ saw you ___ com - ing. _____

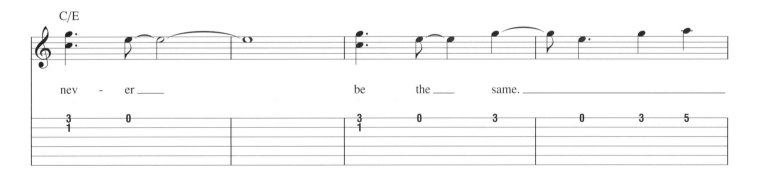

And I'll

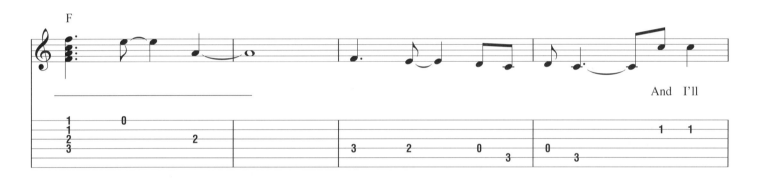

nev - er ___ be the ___ same. _____

D.S. al Fine

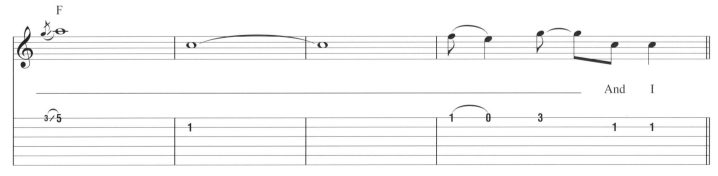

And I

Red

Words and Music by Taylor Swift

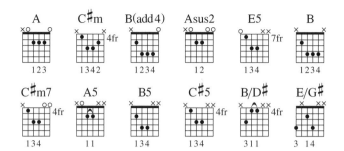

Strum Pattern: 5
Pick Pattern: 5

Intro
Moderately

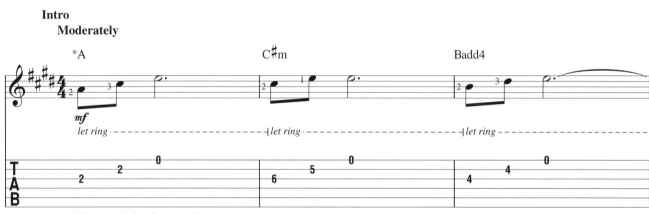

*Chord symbols reflect overall harmony.

Verse

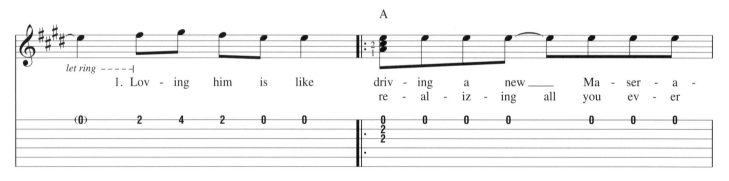

1. Lov - ing him is like driv - ing a new ___ Ma - ser - a -
re - al - iz - ing all you ev - er

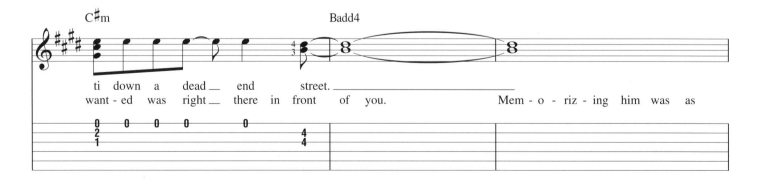

ti down a dead ___ end street. ___
want - ed was right ___ there in front of you. Mem - o - riz - ing him was as

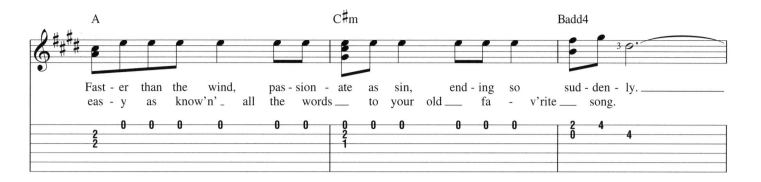

Fast - er than the wind, pas - sion - ate as sin, end - ing so sud - den - ly. _____
eas - y as know'n' _ all the words _ to your old _ fa - v'rite _ song.

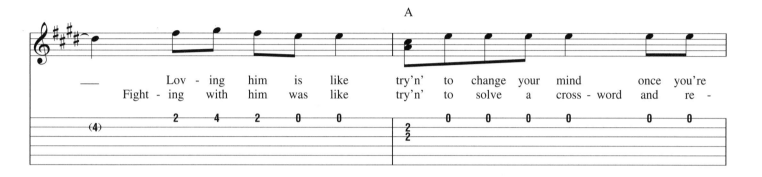

_____ Lov - ing him is like try'n' to change your mind once you're
Fight - ing with him was like try'n' to solve a cross - word and re -

al - read - y fly'n' _ through the free _____ fall, _____ like the
al - iz - in' there's no right an - swer. _____ Re - gret - ting him was like

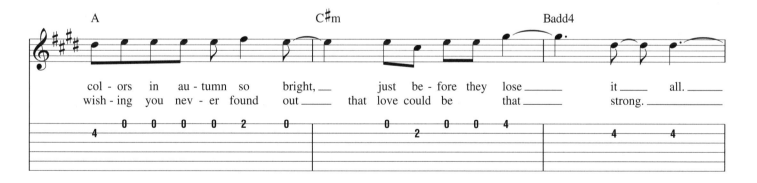

col - ors in au - tumn so bright, _ just be - fore they lose _____ it _ all. _____
wish - ing you nev - er found out _____ that love could be that _____ strong. _____

Chorus

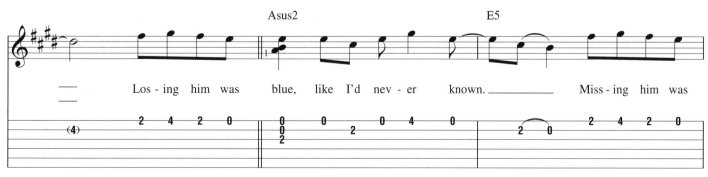

_____ Los - ing him was blue, like I'd nev - er known. _____ Miss - ing him was

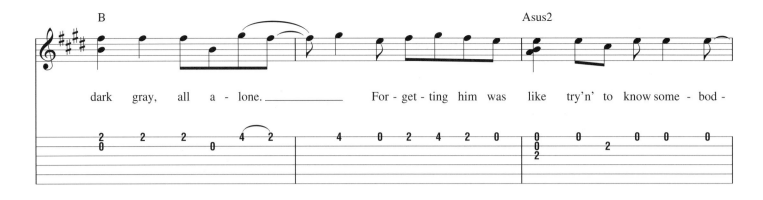

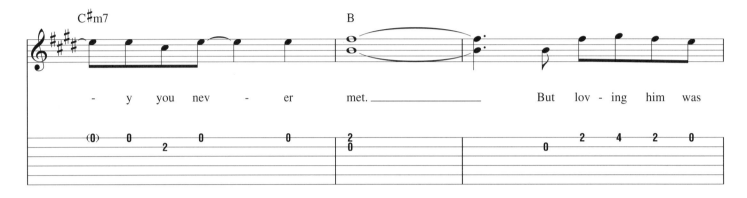

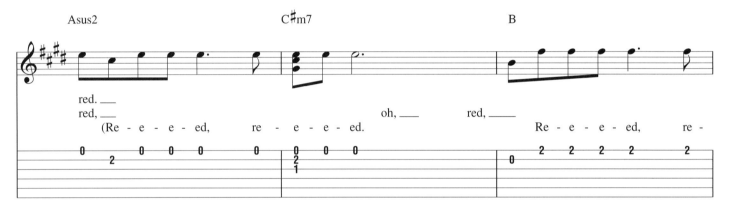

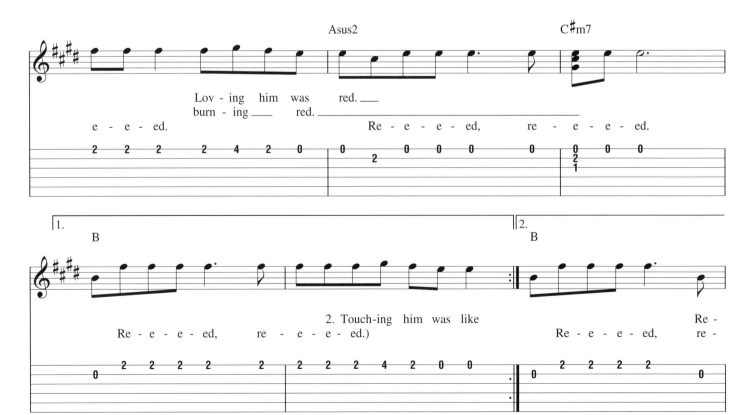

Bridge

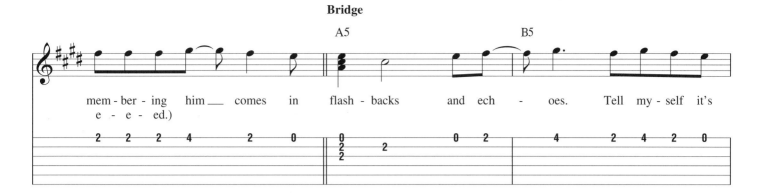

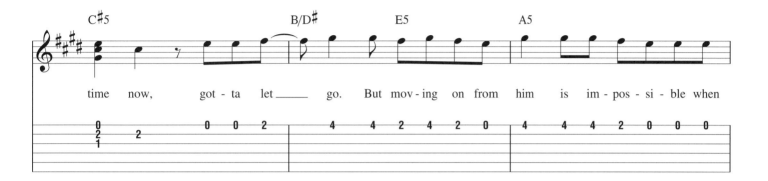

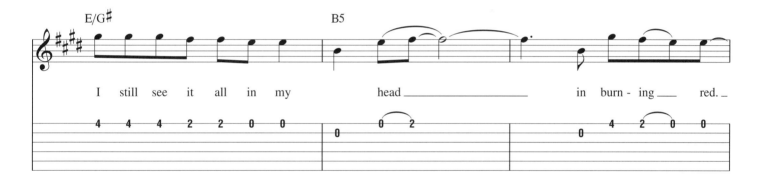

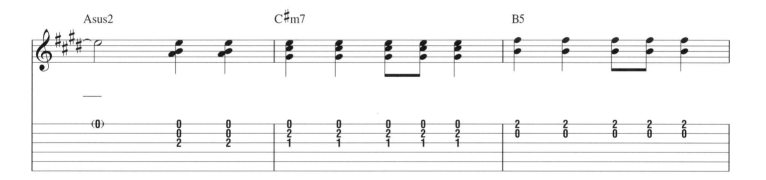

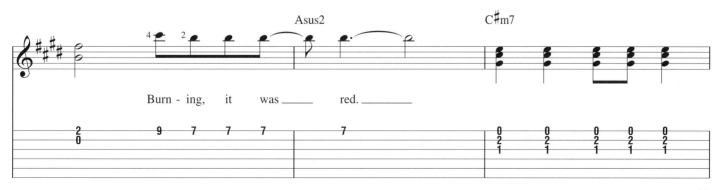

Oh, los-ing him was blue like I'd nev-er known.

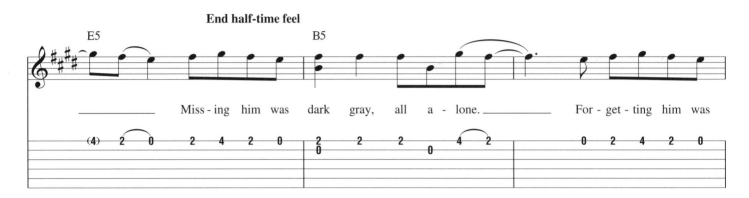

_____ Miss-ing him was dark gray, all a-lone. _____ For-get-ting him was

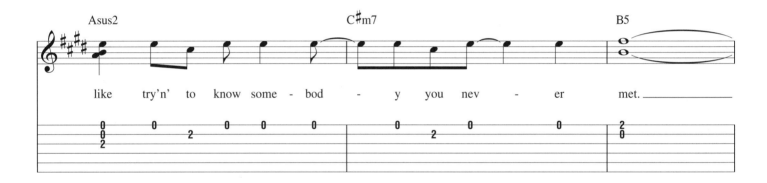

like try'n' to know some-bod - y you nev - er met. _____

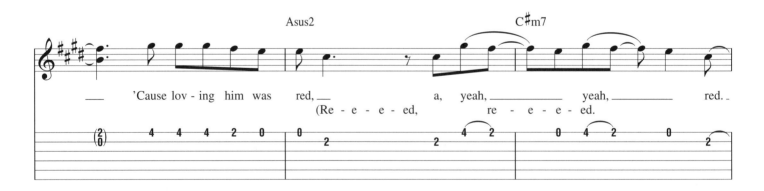

_ 'Cause lov-ing him was red, _ a, yeah, _____ yeah, _____ red.
(Re - e - e - ed, re - e - e - ed.

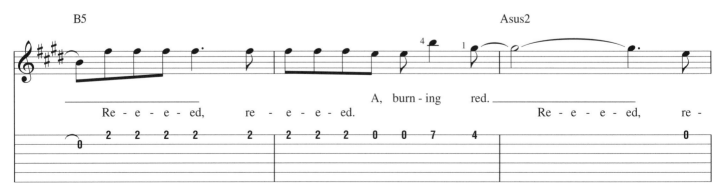

_____ A, burn-ing red. _____
Re - e - e - ed, re - e - e - ed. Re - e - ed, re -

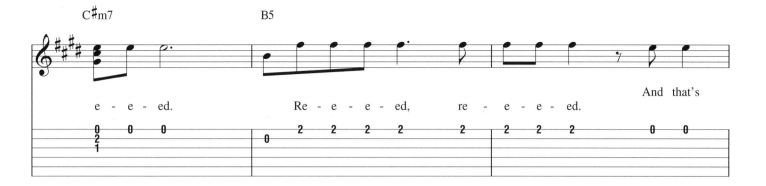

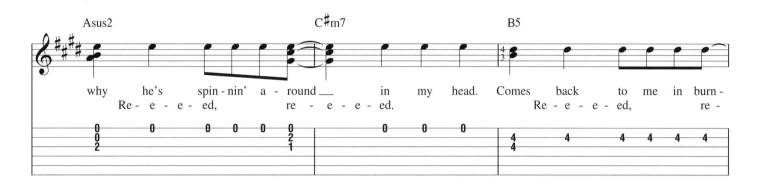

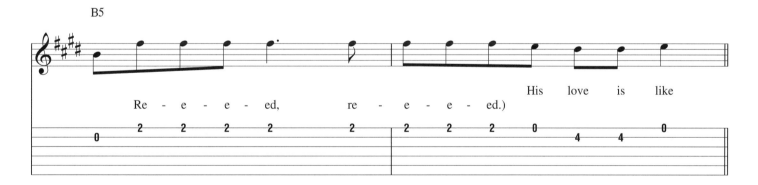

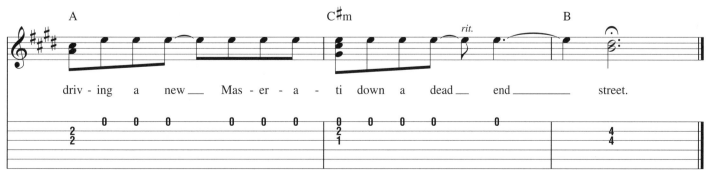

Treacherous

Words and Music by Taylor Swift and Dan Wilson

Strum Pattern: 1
Pick Pattern: 4

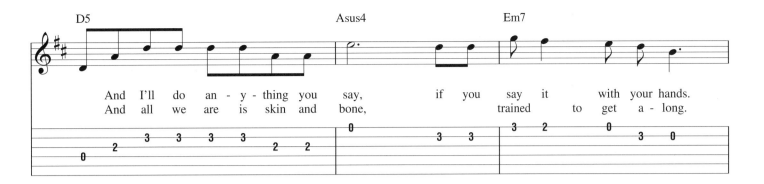

And I'll do an-y-thing you say, if you say it with your hands.
And all we are is skin and bone, trained to get a-long.

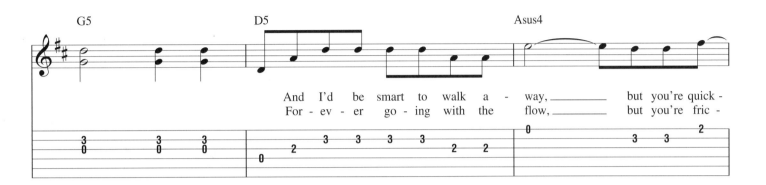

And I'd be smart to walk a-way, _____ but you're quick -
For-ev-er go-ing with the flow, _____ but you're fric -

Chorus

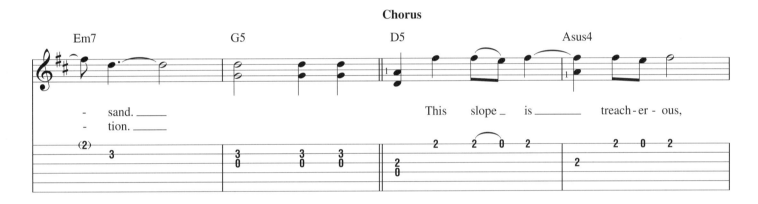

- sand. _____
- tion. _____

This slope ___ is _____ treach-er-ous,

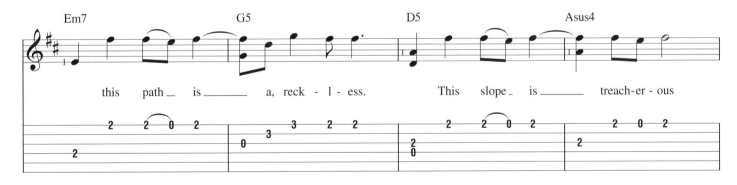

this path ___ is _____ a, reck-l-ess.   This slope ___ is _____ treach-er-ous

1.

Interlude

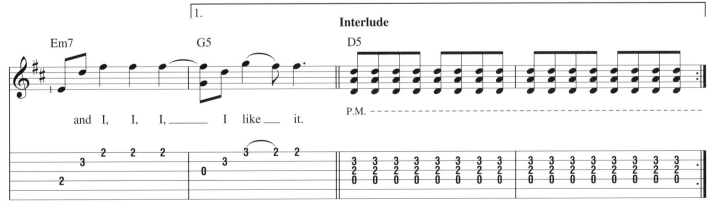

and I, I, I, _____ I like ___ it.   P.M. -------------------------------------

23

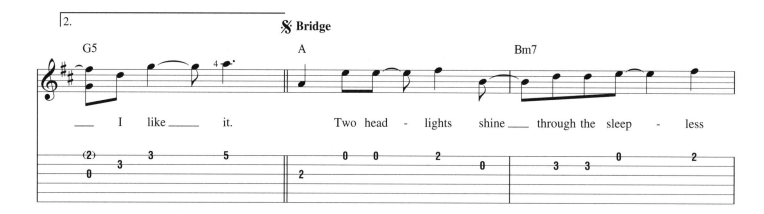

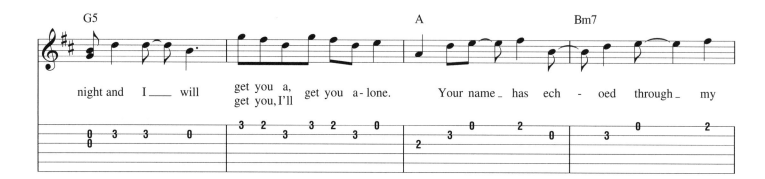

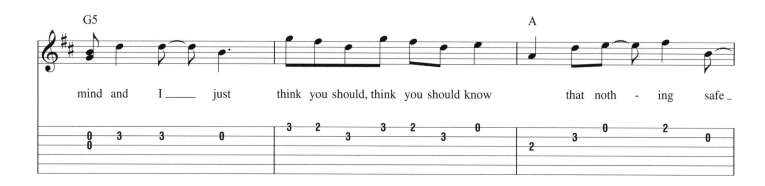

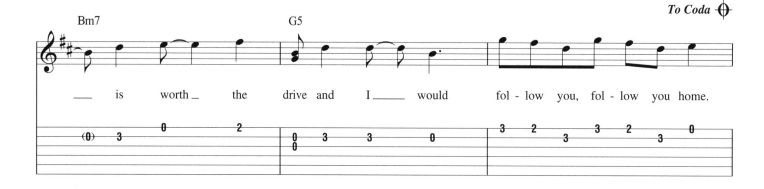

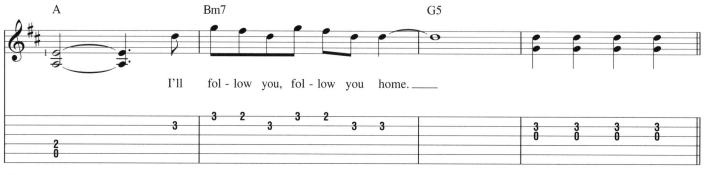

Chorus

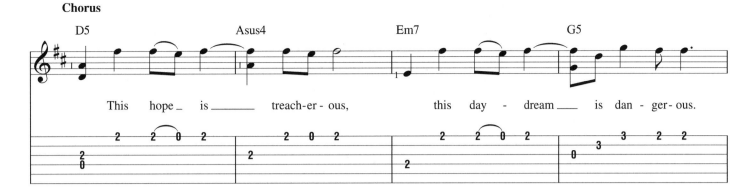

This hope _ is _____ treach-er-ous, this day - dream ___ is dan-ger-ous.

D.S. al Coda

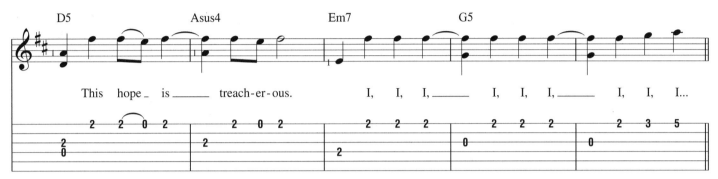

This hope _ is _____ treach-er-ous. I, I, I, _____ I, I, I, _____ I, I, I...

Coda

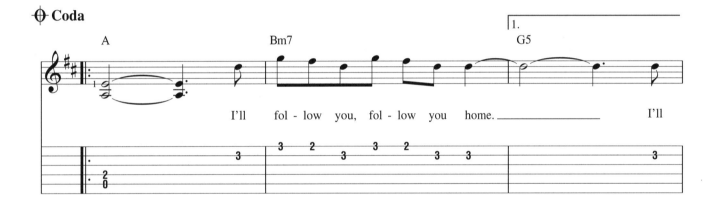

I'll fol - low you, fol - low you home. _____ I'll

Outro

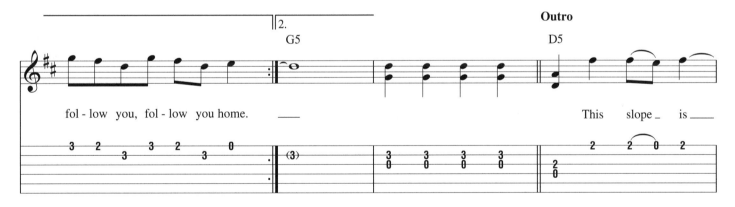

fol - low you, fol - low you home. ___ This slope _ is ___

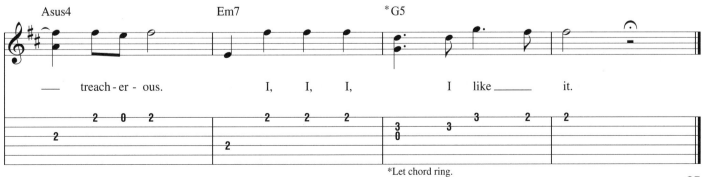

___ treach - er - ous. I, I, I, I like _____ it.

*Let chord ring.

All Too Well

Words and Music by Taylor Swift and Liz Rose

Strum Pattern: 1
Pick Pattern: 4

1. I walked through the door _ with you, the air was cold. _

Some-thin' 'bout it felt __ like home __ some - how. _ And I left my scarf _ there at your

sis - ter's house, _ and you've ___ still got it in your drawer e - ven now.

*Let chord ring.

Interlude

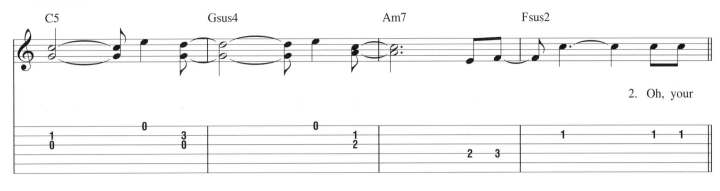

2. Oh, your

% Verse

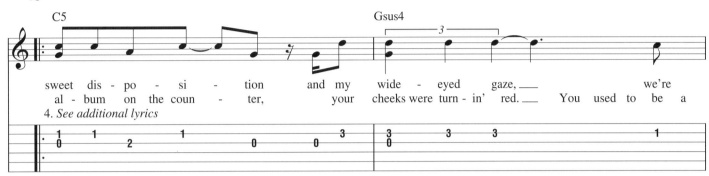

sweet dis - po - si - tion and my wide - eyed gaze, ___ we're
al - bum on the coun - ter, your cheeks were turn - in' red. ___ You used to be a
4. See additional lyrics

sing - in' in the car ___ get - tin' lost ___ up - state. Au - tumn leaves ___ fall - in' down like
lit - tle kid with glass - es in a twin - size bed. ___ And your moth - er's tell - in' sto - ries 'bout you on the

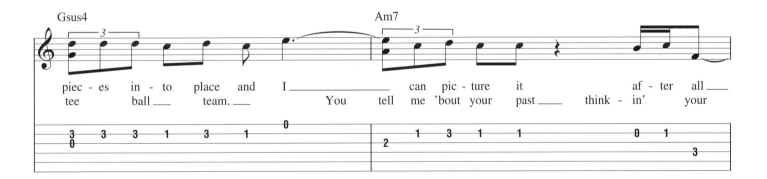

piec - es in - to place and I ___ can pic - ture it af - ter all ___
tee ball ___ team. ___ You tell me 'bout your past ___ think - in' your

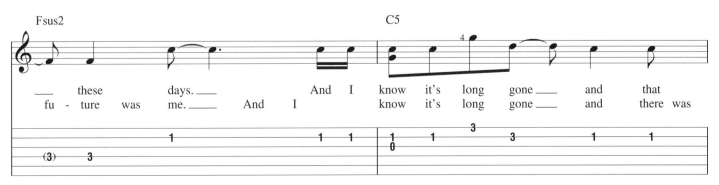

___ these days. ___ And I know it's long gone ___ and that
fu - ture was me. ___ And I know it's long gone ___ and there was

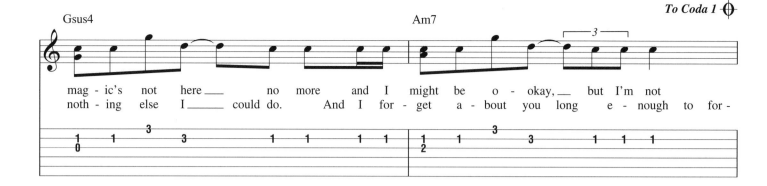

mag - ic's not here ___ no more and I might be o - okay, ___ but I'm not
noth - ing else I ___ could do. And I for - get a - bout you long e - nough to for-

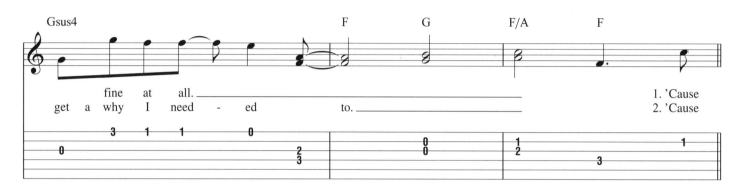

fine at all. ___
get a why I need - ed to. ___

1. 'Cause
2. 'Cause

***%.%.* Chorus**

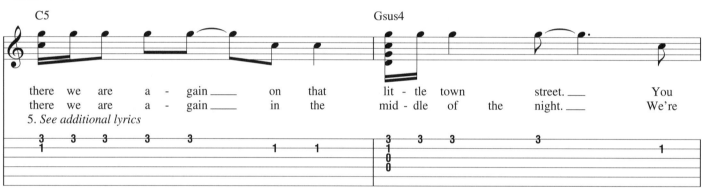

there we are a - gain ___ on that lit - tle town street. ___ You
there we are a - gain ___ in the mid - dle of the night. ___ We're

5. See additional lyrics

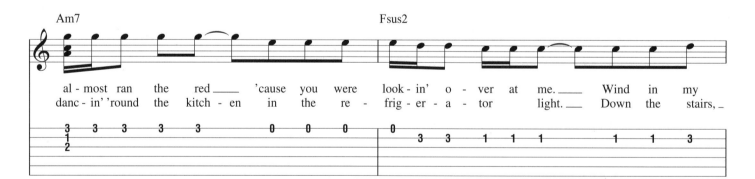

al - most ran the red ___ 'cause you were look - in' o - ver at me. ___ Wind in my
danc - in' 'round the kitch - en in the re - frig - er - a - tor light. ___ Down the stairs, ___

To Coda 2 1.

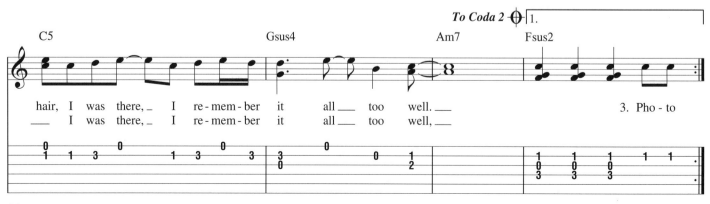

hair, I was there, ___ I re - mem - ber it all ___ too well. ___
___ I was there, ___ I re - mem - ber it all ___ too well,

3. Pho - to

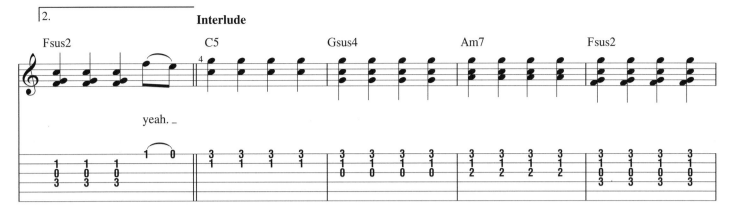

Interlude

Chorus

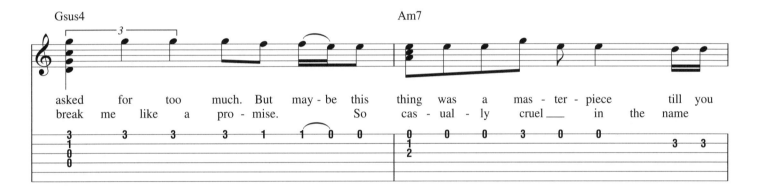

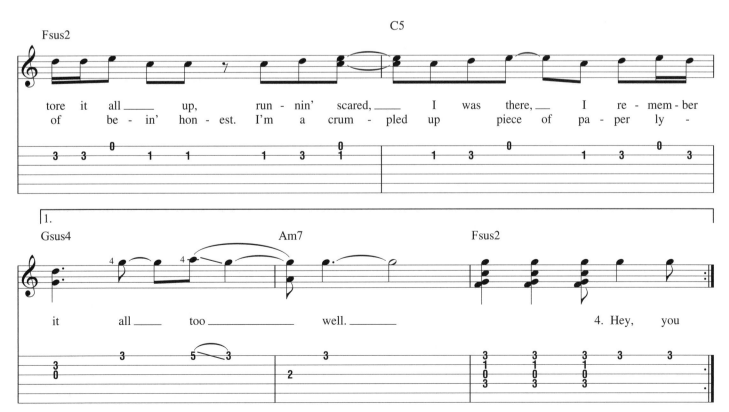

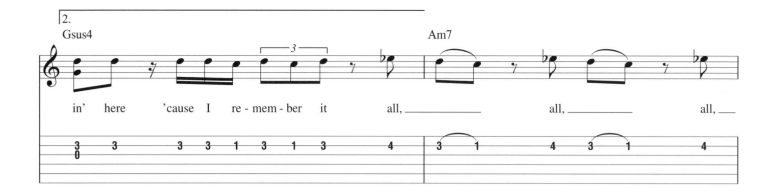

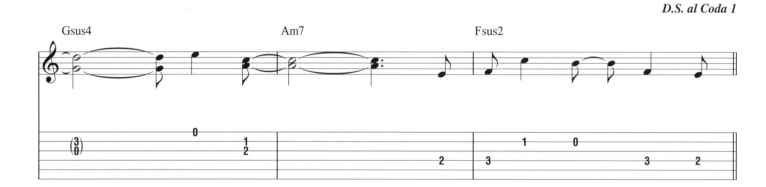

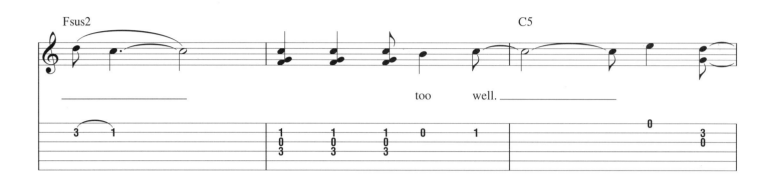

Coda 1

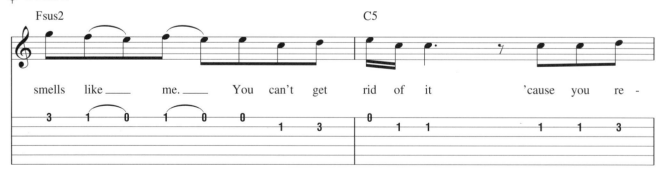

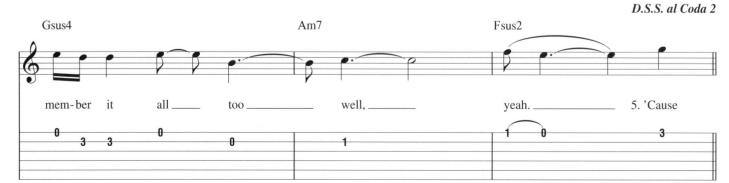

Coda 2

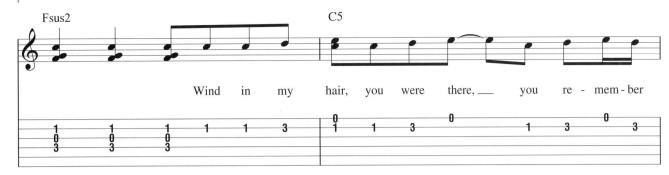

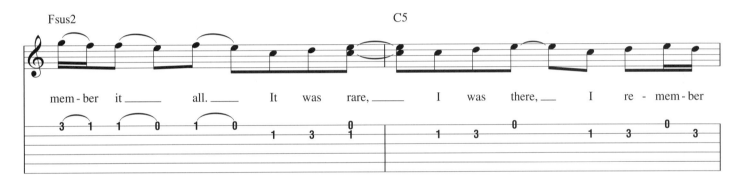

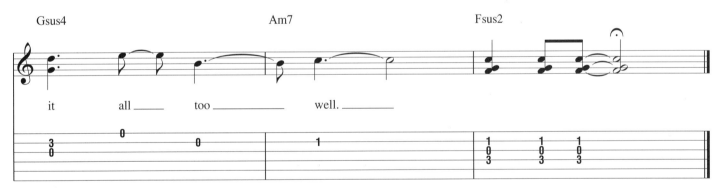

Additional Lyrics

4. Time won't fly, it's like I'm paralyzed by it.
I'd like to be my old self again, but I'm still try'n' to find it.
After plaid shirt days and nights when you made me your own,
Now you mail back my things and I walk home alone.
But you keep my old scarf from that very first week
'Cause it reminds you of innocence and it smells like me.
You can't get rid of it
'Cause you remember it all too well, yeah.

Chorus 5. 'Cause there we are again when I loved you so
Back before you lost the one real thing you've ever known.
It was rare, I was there, I remember it all too well.
Wind in my hair, you were there, you remember it all.
Down the stairs, you were there, 'cause you remember it all.
It was rare, I was there, I remember it all too well.

22

Words and Music by Taylor Swift, Shellback and Max Martin

Strum Pattern: 5
Pick Pattern: 5

Intro
Moderately, in 2

Verse

1. It feels like a per-fect night to dress up like hip-sters
2. It seems like one of those nights. This place is too crowd-ed.

and make fun of our ex-es. Ah, ah. ___ Ah, ah.
Too man-y cool ___ kids. Ah, ah. ___ Ah, ah.

It feels like a per-fect night for break-fast at mid-night
It seems like one of those nights we ditch the whole scene

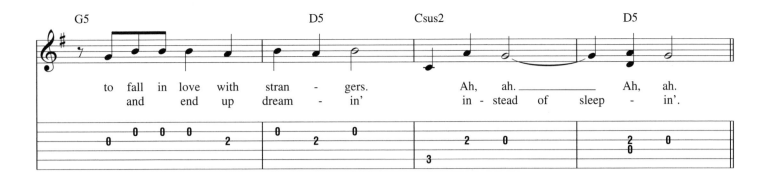

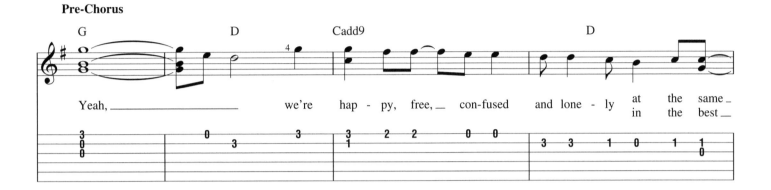

Pre-Chorus

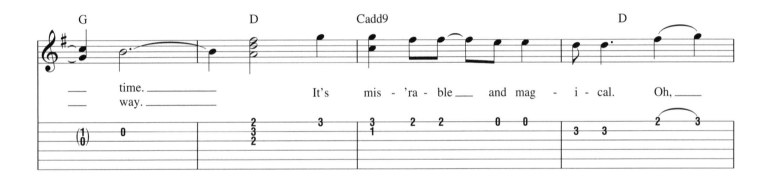

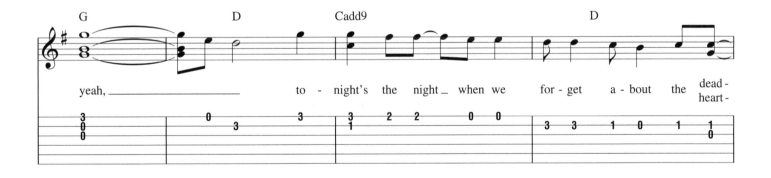

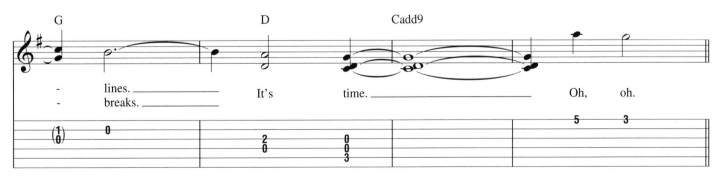

I don't know a-bout you, but I'm feel - in' twen - ty two. _____

*Sung one octave higher throughout Chorus and Bridge.

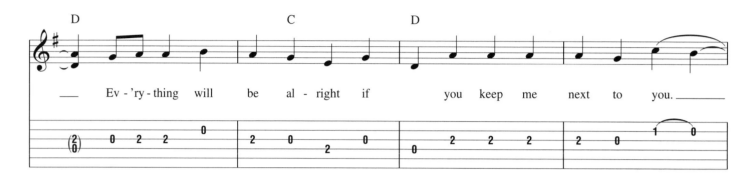

_____ Ev - 'ry - thing will be al - right if you keep me next to you. _____

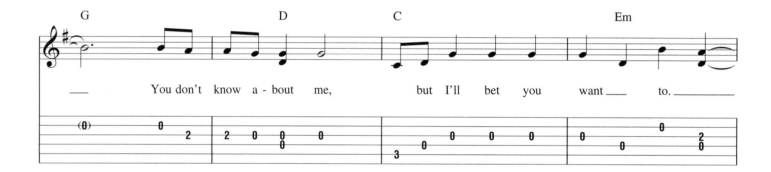

_____ You don't know a - bout me, but I'll bet you want ___ to. _____

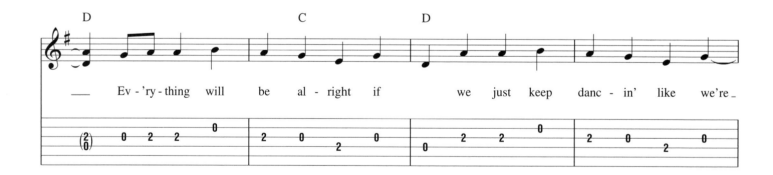

_____ Ev - 'ry - thing will be al - right if we just keep danc - in' like we're_

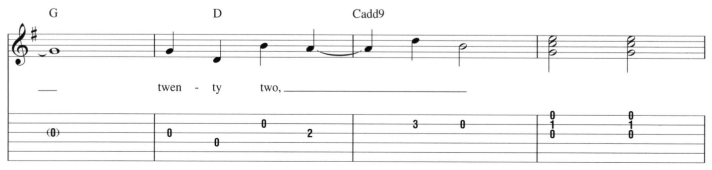

_____ twen - ty two, _____

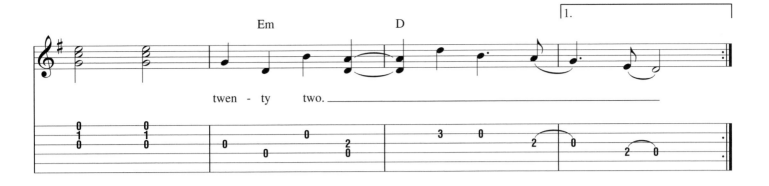

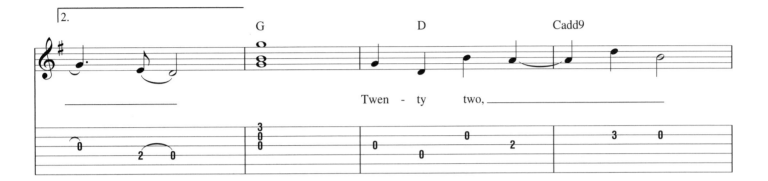

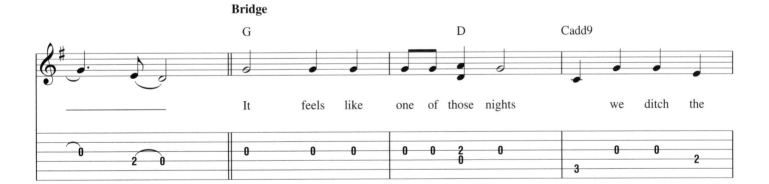

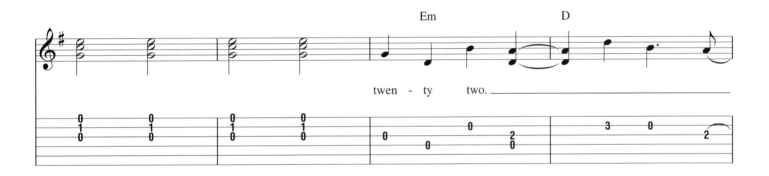

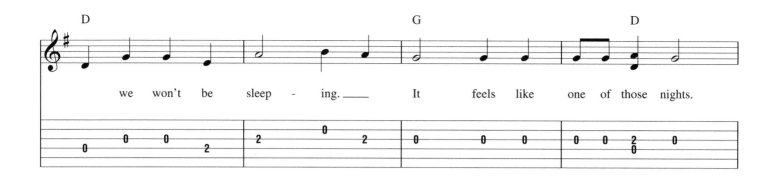

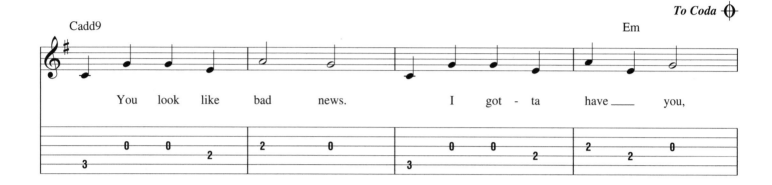

To Coda ⊕

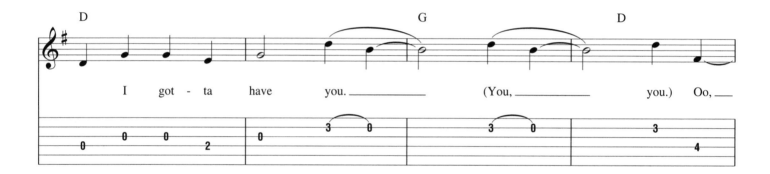

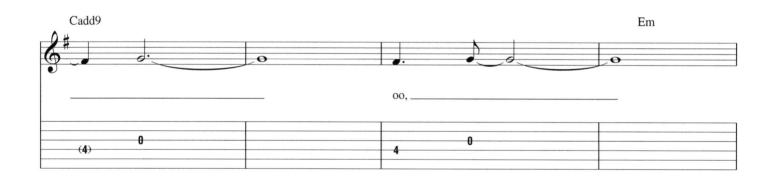

D.S. al Coda
(take 2nd ending)

⊕ **Coda**

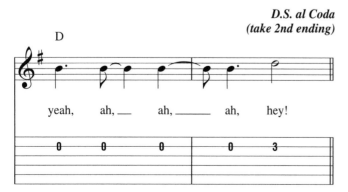

We Are Never Ever Getting Back Together

Words and Music by Taylor Swift, Shellback and Max Martin

Strum Pattern: 5
Pick Pattern: 1

*Knock on guitar body w/ right hand.

1. I re-mem-ber when we broke up the first time, say-ing, "This is it. I've had e-nough." 'Cause like, we had-n't seen each oth-er in a month when you said you need-ed space. **Spoken: What? Then you come a-round a-gain and say, "Ba-by, I real-ly gon-na miss you pick-ing fights. And me,

**Lyrics in italics are spoken throughout.

miss you and I swear I'm gon-na change, *trust me."* Re - mem - ber how that last - ed for a
fall - ing for it, scream - ing that I'm right. And you would hide a - way and find your peace of

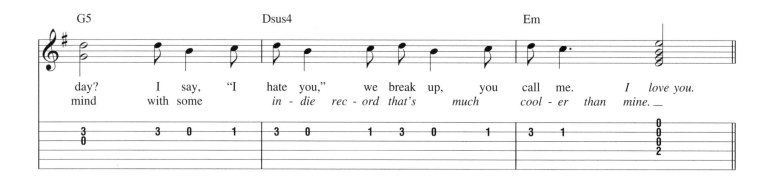

day? I say, "I hate you," we break up, you call me. *I love you.*
mind with some *in - die rec - ord that's much cool - er than mine.*

Pre-Chorus

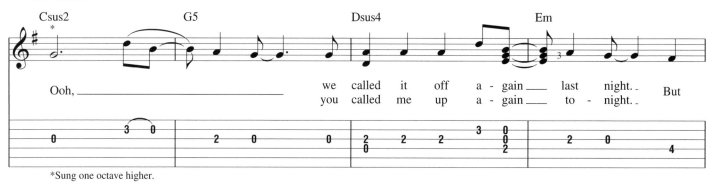

Ooh, _____ we called it off a - gain ___ last night. But
you called me up a - gain ___ to - night.

*Sung one octave higher.

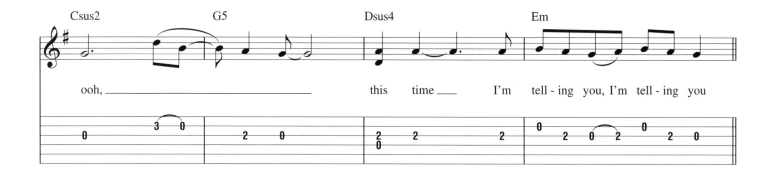

ooh, _____ this time ___ I'm tell - ing you, I'm tell - ing you

Chorus

we are nev - er ev - er ev - er _____ get - ting back to - geth - er.

We _____ are nev - er ev - er ev - er _____ get - ting back to - geth - er.

You go talk to your ___ friends, talk to my ___ friends, talk to me. ___ But

1.

we _____ are nev - er ev - er ev - er _____ ev - er get - ting back to -

Interlude

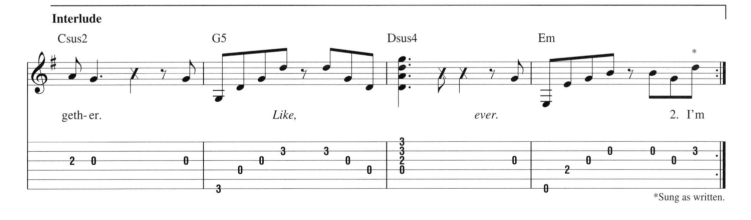

geth - er. *Like,* *ever.* 2. I'm

*Sung as written.

2.   **Interlude**

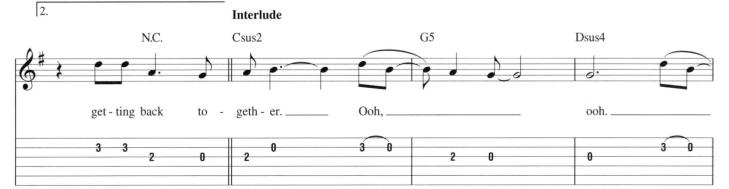

get - ting back to - geth - er. _____ Ooh, _____ ooh. _____

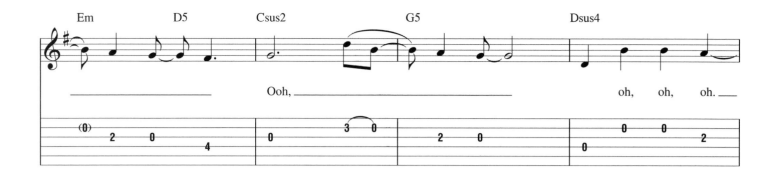

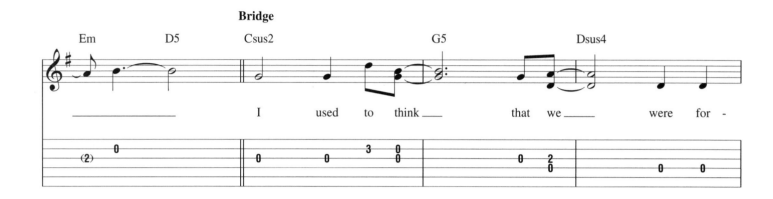

Bridge

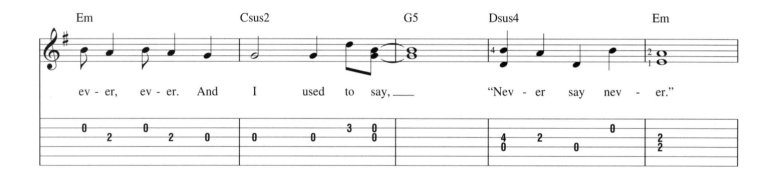

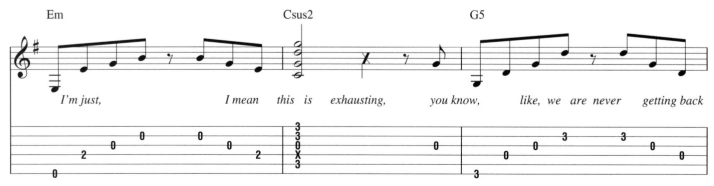

Chorus

together, like ever. No. We are nev - er, ev - er, ev - er

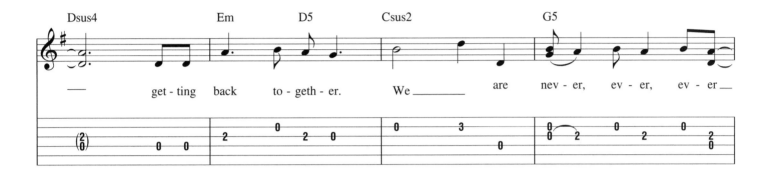

— get - ting back to - geth - er. We are nev - er, ev - er, ev - er

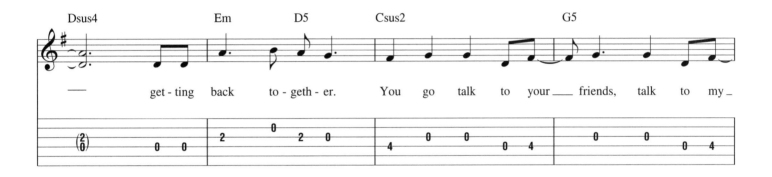

— get - ting back to - geth - er. You go talk to your friends, talk to my

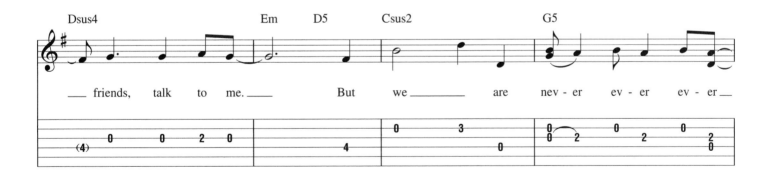

— friends, talk to me. But we are nev - er ev - er ev - er

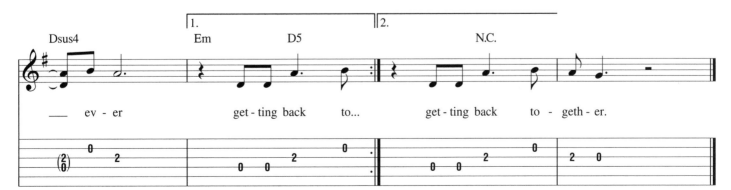

— ev - er   get - ting back to...   get - ting back to - geth - er.

I Almost Do

Words and Music by Taylor Swift

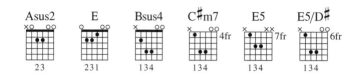

Strum Pattern: 5
Pick Pattern: 5

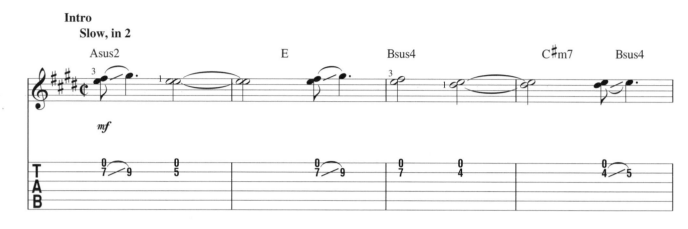

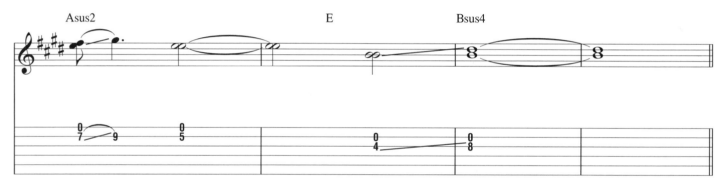

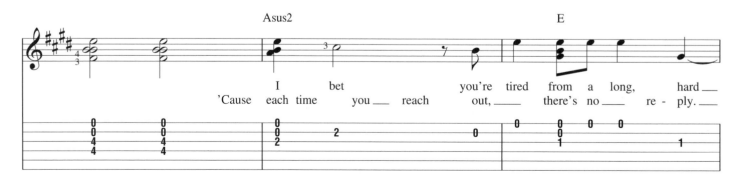

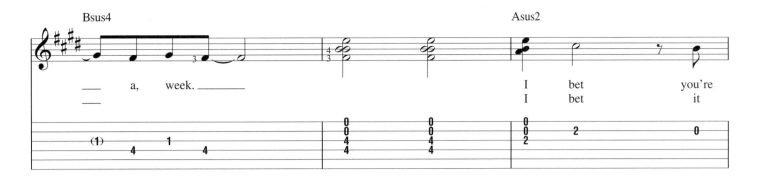

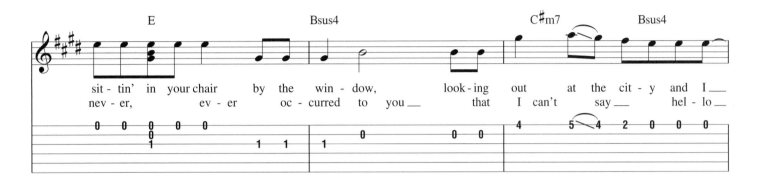

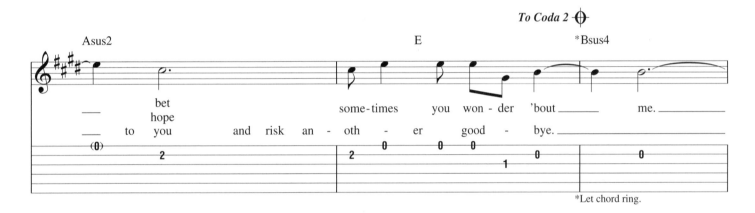

*Let chord ring.

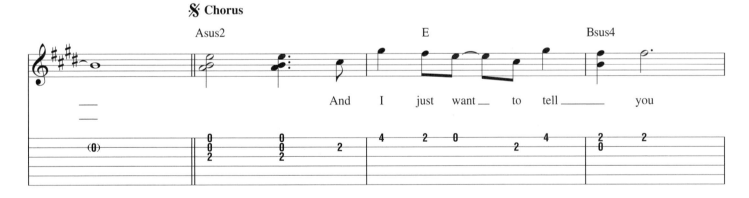

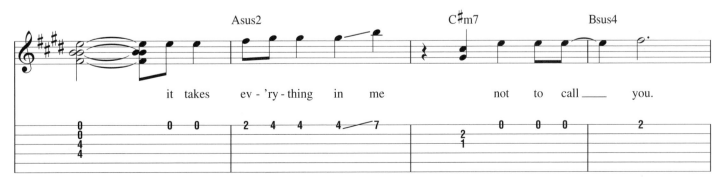

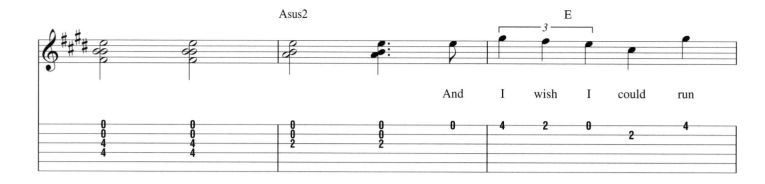

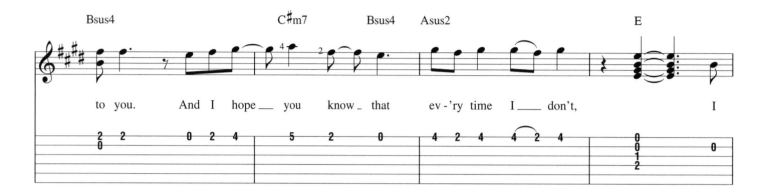

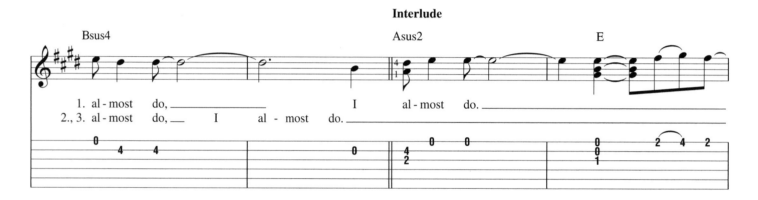

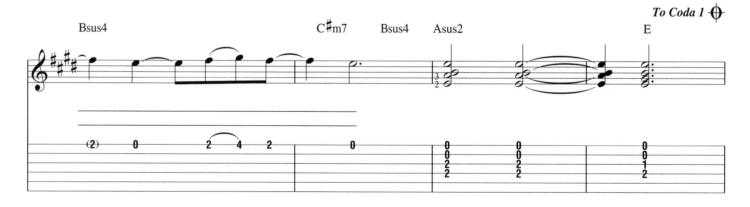

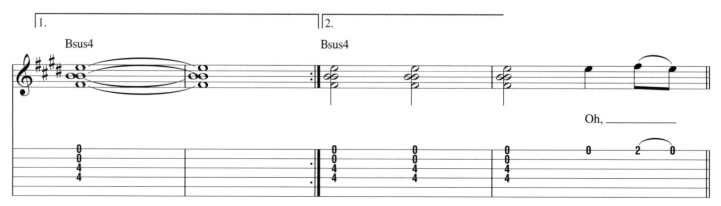

Bridge

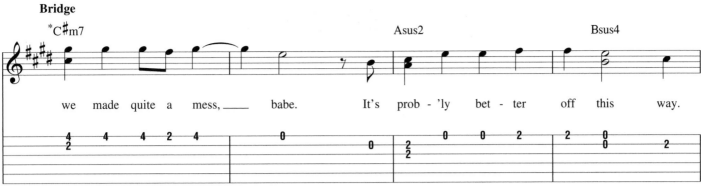

*C#m7   Asus2   Bsus4

we made quite a mess,____ babe. It's prob - 'ly bet - ter off this way.

*Let chord ring.

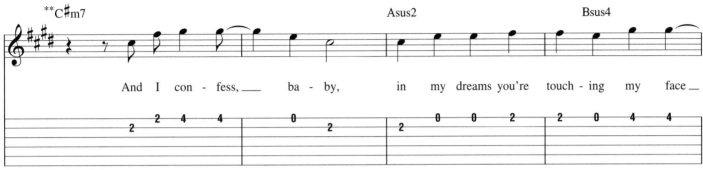

**C#m7   Asus2   Bsus4

And I con - fess,____ ba - by, in my dreams you're touch - ing my face____

**Let chord ring.

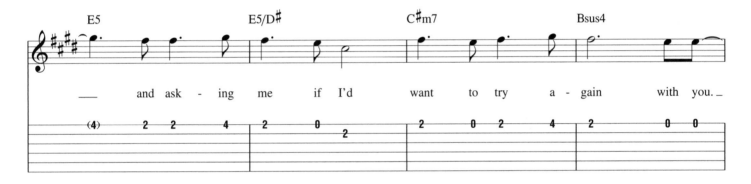

E5   E5/D#   C#m7   Bsus4

____ and ask - ing me if I'd want to try a - gain with you.__

D.S. al Coda 1

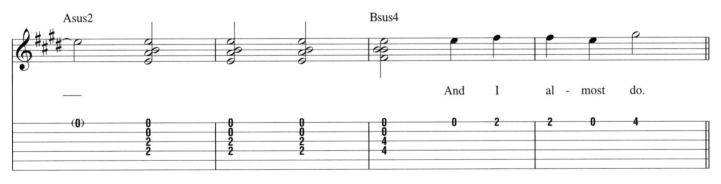

Asus2   Bsus4

____ And I al - most do.

⊕ **Coda 1**   *D.S.S. al Coda 2*   ⊕ **Coda 2**

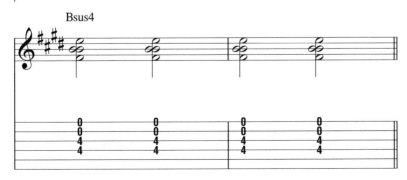

Bsus4

Bsus4

rit.

____ me.

Stay Stay Stay

Words and Music by Taylor Swift

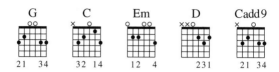

*Capo V

Strum Pattern: 5
Pick Pattern: 1

Intro
Fast

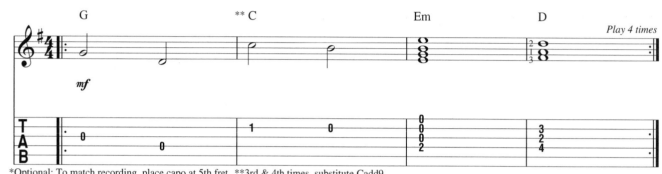

*Optional: To match recording, place capo at 5th fret. **3rd & 4th times, substitute Cadd9.

Verse

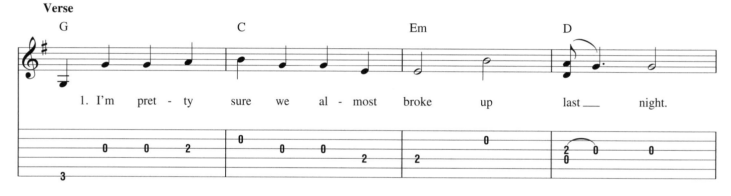

1. I'm pret-ty sure we al-most broke up last ___ night.

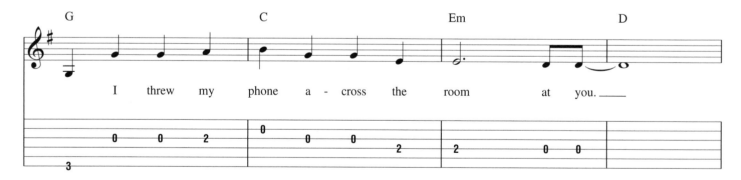

I threw my phone a-cross the room at you. ___

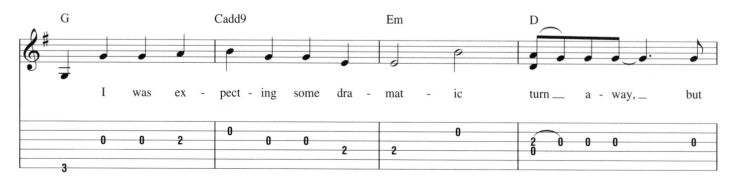

I was ex-pect-ing some dra-mat-ic turn ___ a-way, ___ but

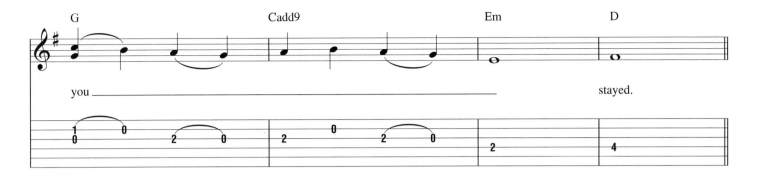

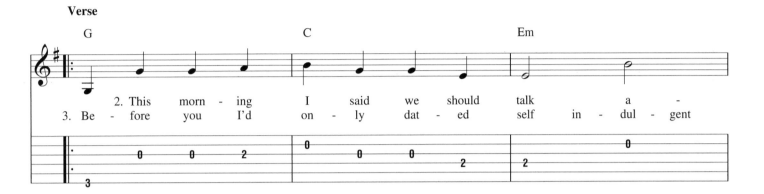

Verse

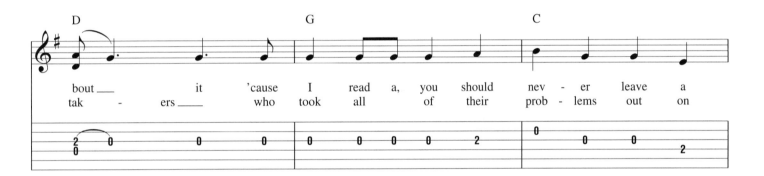

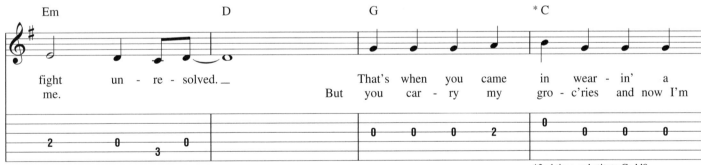

*2nd time, substitute Cadd9.

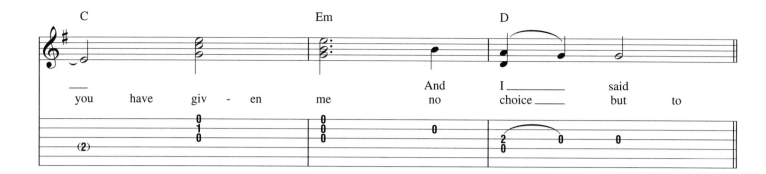

C   Em   D

you have giv - en me   no   And I ___ choice ___ said but to

Chorus

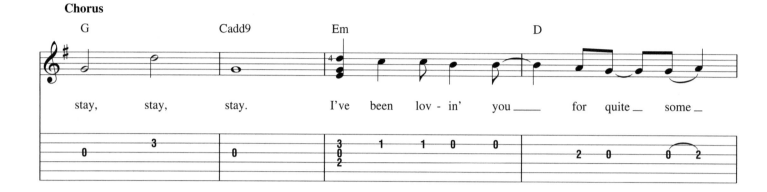

G   Cadd9   Em   D

stay, stay, stay. I've been lov - in' you ___ for quite ___ some ___

G   Cadd9   Em   D

time, time, time. You think that it's fun - ny when ___ I'm ___

G   Cadd9   Em   D

mad, mad, mad. But I think that it's best ___ if we ___ both ___

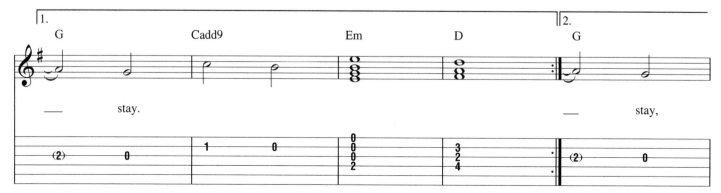

1.
G   Cadd9   Em   D   2.   G

___ stay.   ___ stay,

*Let chords ring, next 4 meas.

**Let chords ring, next 4 meas.

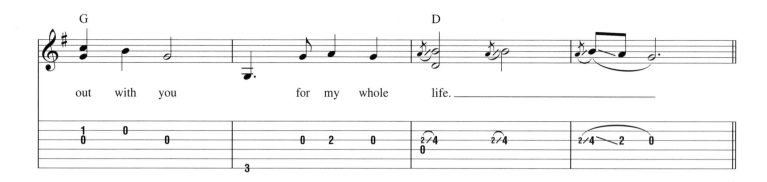

out with you   for my whole   life._____

Chorus

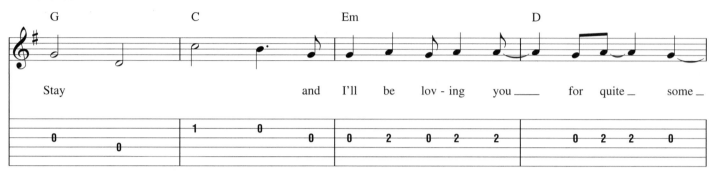

Stay   and I'll be lov-ing you___ for quite___ some___

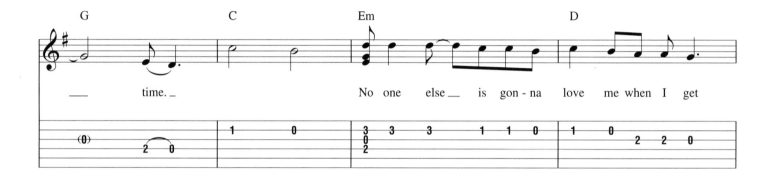

___   time.___   No one else___ is gon-na love me when I get

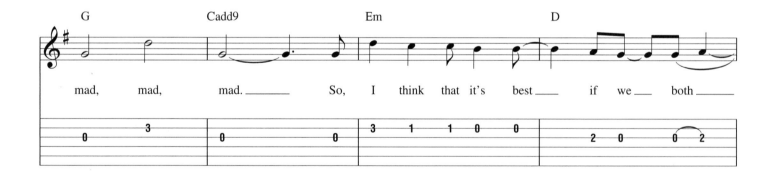

mad,   mad,   mad._____ So, I think that it's best___ if we___ both_____

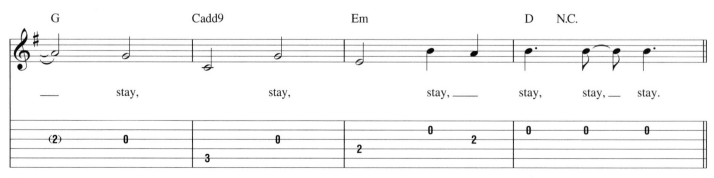

___   stay,   stay,   stay,___ stay, stay,___ stay.

Outro-Chorus

Stay, stay, stay. I've been lov-in' you ___ for quite ___ some ___

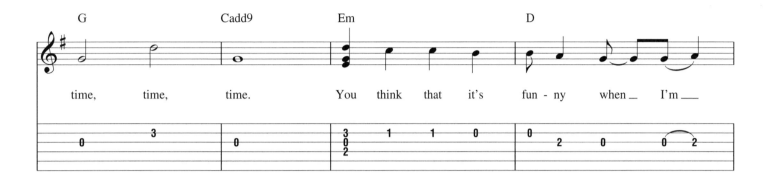

time, time, time. You think that it's fun-ny when ___ I'm ___

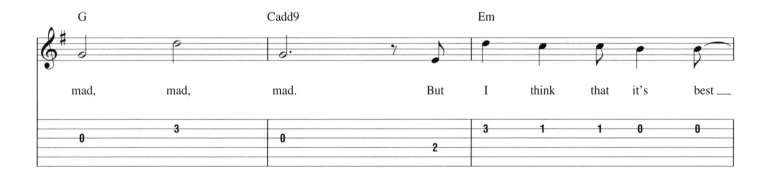

mad, mad, mad. But I think that it's best ___

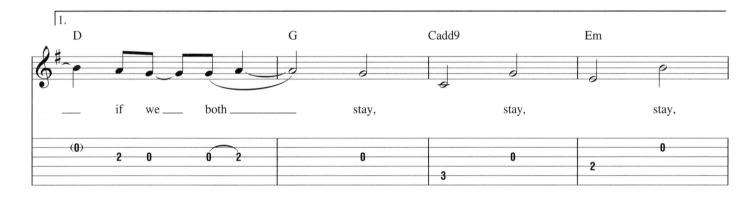

___ if we ___ both _____ stay, stay, stay,

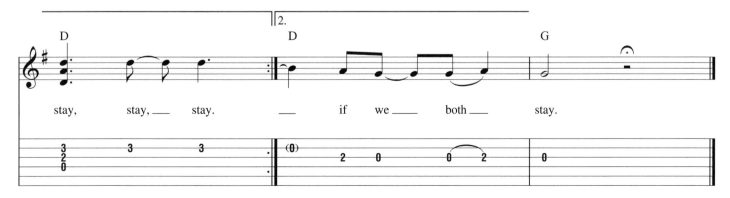

stay, stay, ___ stay. ___ if we ___ both ___ stay.

The Last Time

Words and Music by Taylor Swift, Garret Lee (Jacknife Lee) and Gary Lightbody

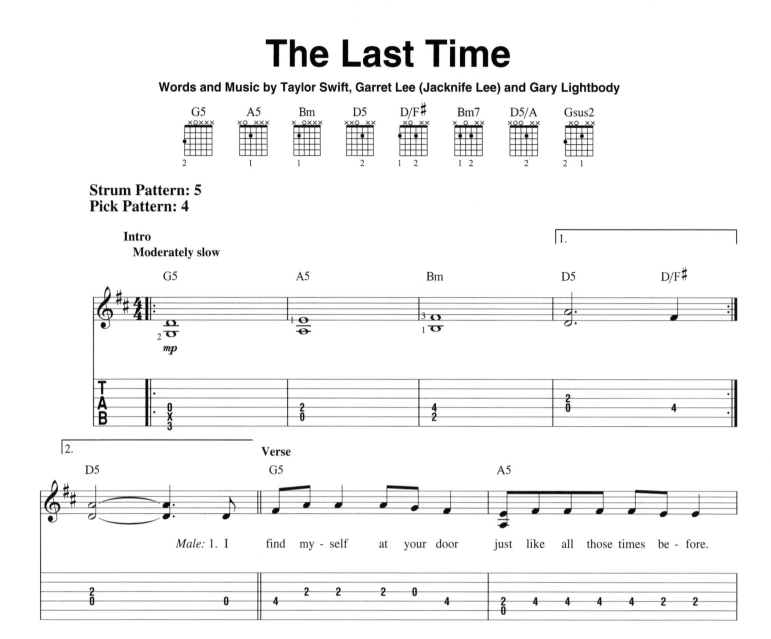

Strum Pattern: 5
Pick Pattern: 4

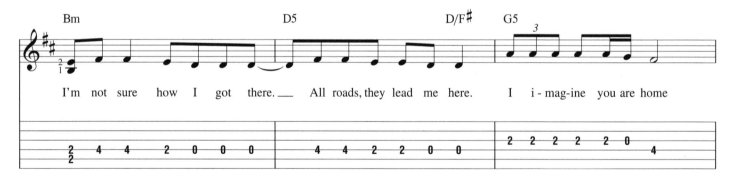

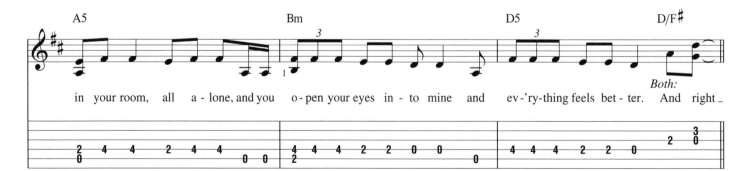

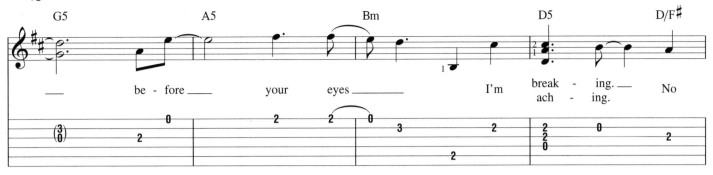

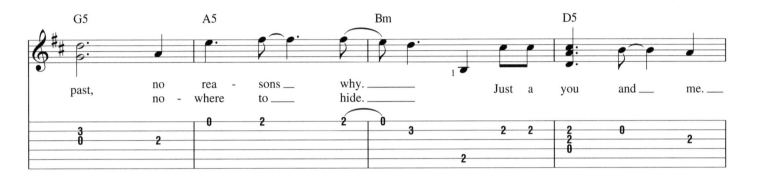

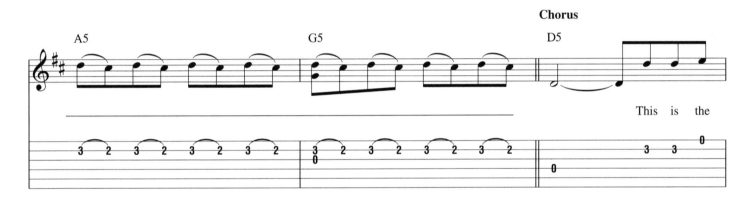

Chorus

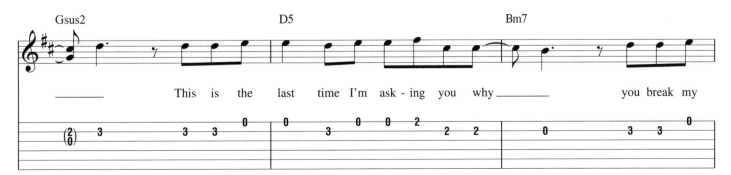

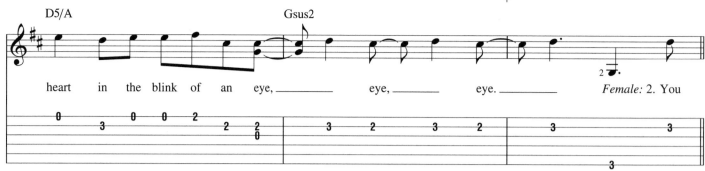

heart   in   the   blink   of   an   eye,_____   eye,_____   eye._____   *Female:* 2. You

Verse

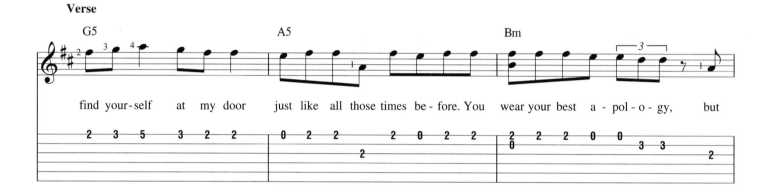

find your-self   at   my door   just   like   all those times be - fore. You   wear your best a - pol - o - gy,   but

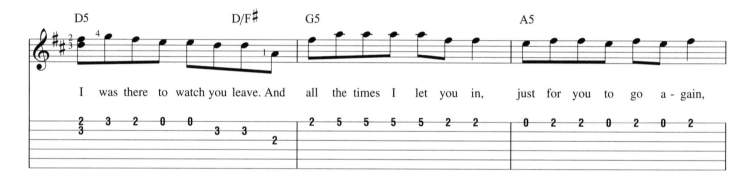

I   was there to watch you leave. And   all   the times I   let you in,   just   for you   to   go a - gain,

D.S. al Coda   ⊕ **Coda**

dis - ap-pear when you come back,   ev -'ry-thing is bet-ter.   And right____

Both:

Interlude

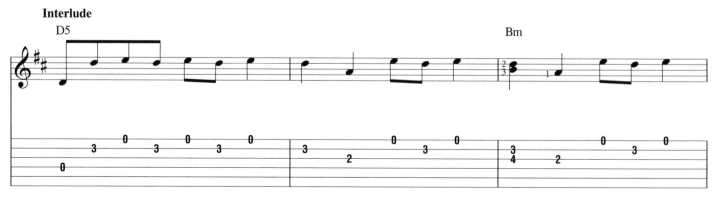

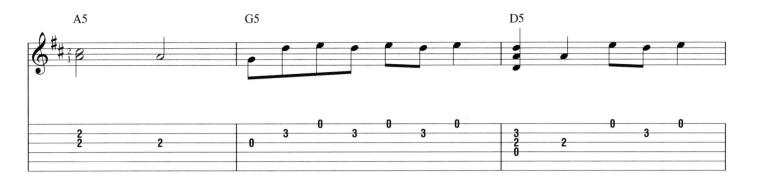

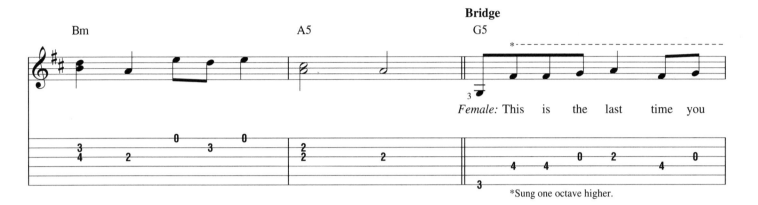

Bridge

Female: This is the last time you

*Sung one octave higher.

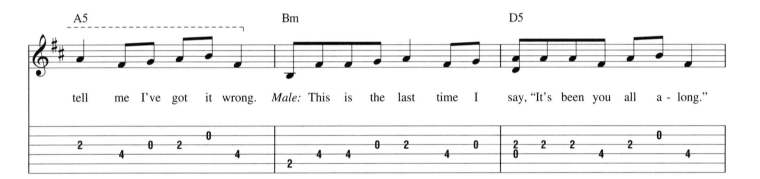

tell me I've got it wrong. *Male:* This is the last time I say, "It's been you all a - long."

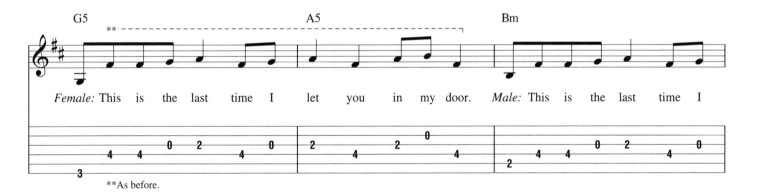

Female: This is the last time I let you in my door. *Male:* This is the last time I

**As before.

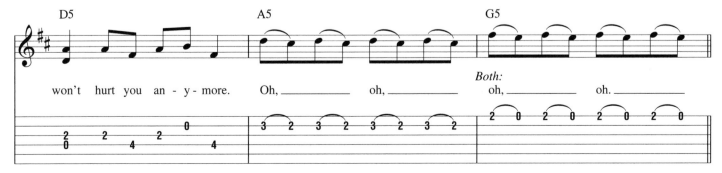

won't hurt you an - y - more. Oh, _____ oh, _____ *Both:* oh, _____ oh. _____

Chorus

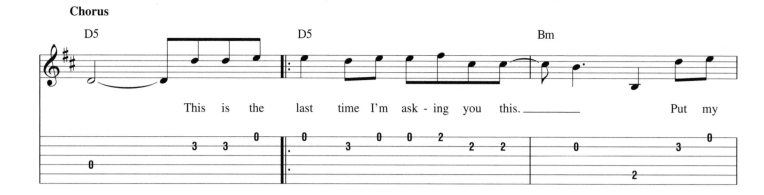

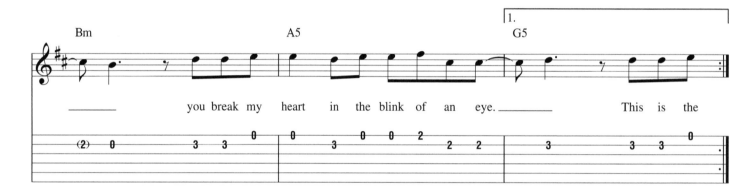

Outro

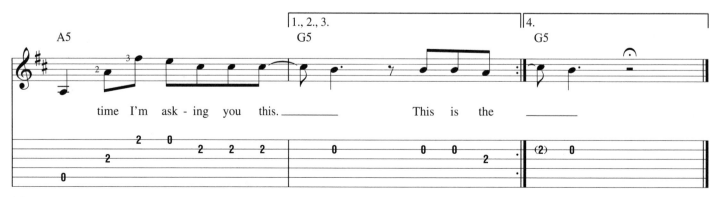

Holy Ground

Words and Music by Taylor Swift

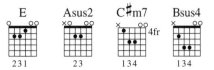

Strum Pattern: 1
Pick Pattern: 1

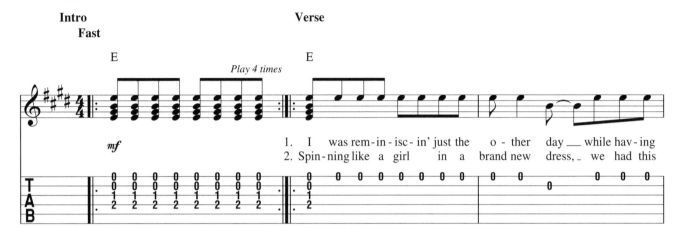

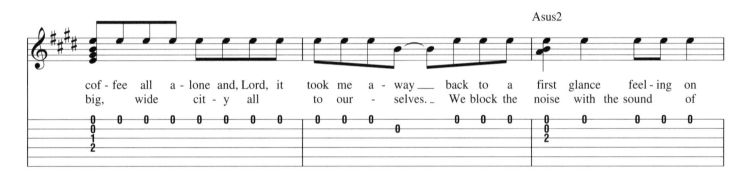

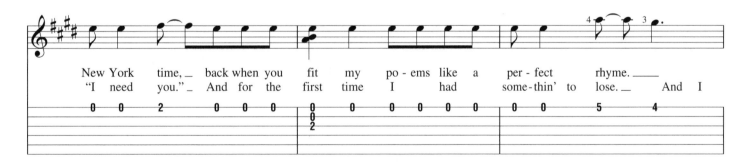

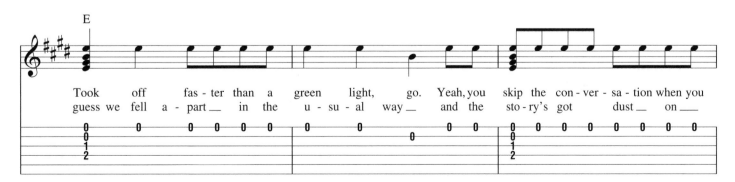

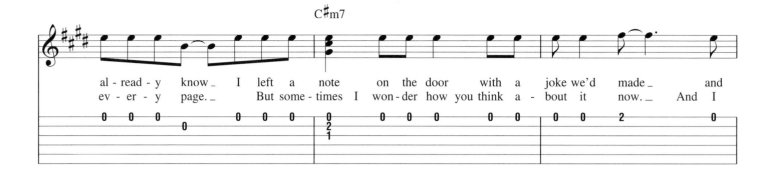

al - read - y know _ I left a note on the door with a joke we'd made _ and
ev - er - y page. _ But some - times I won - der how you think a - bout it now. _ And I

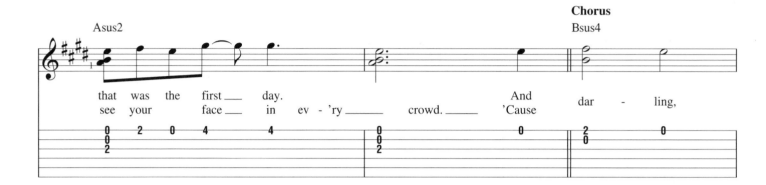

that was the first ___ day. And dar - ling,
see your face ___ in ev - 'ry ___ crowd. ___ 'Cause

Chorus

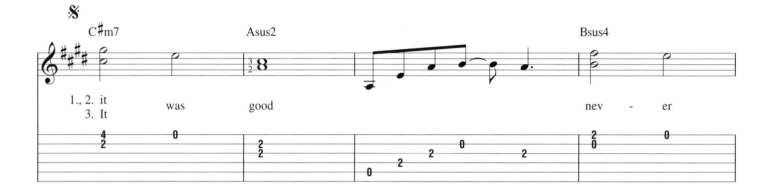

1., 2. it was good nev - er
3. It

look - ing down. And right there

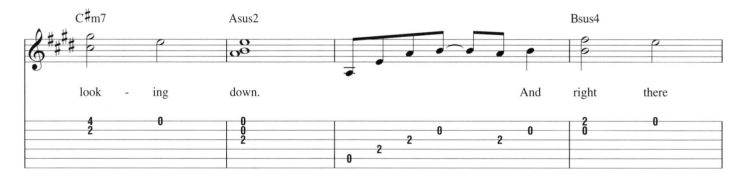

Interlude

where we stood was ho - ly ground. _____

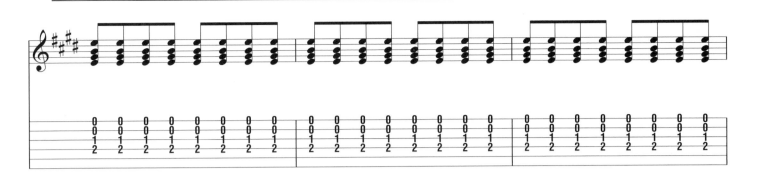

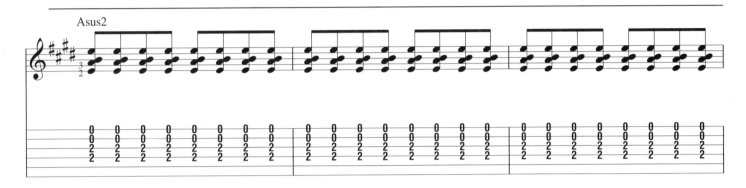

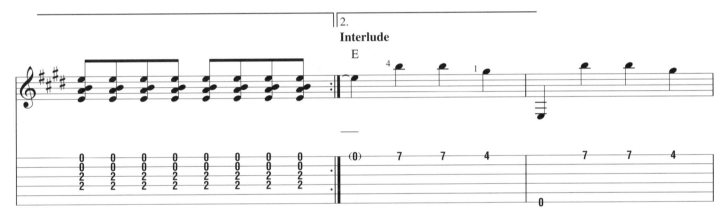

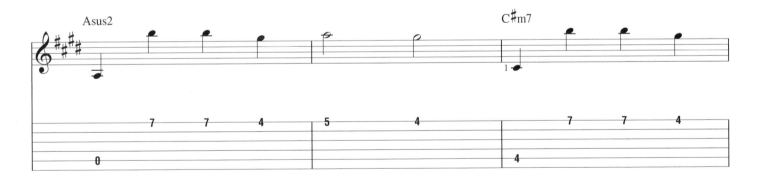

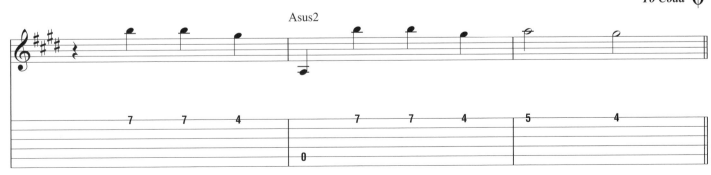

Bridge

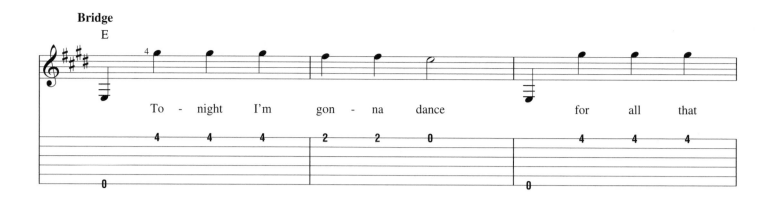

To - night I'm gon - na dance for all that

we've been through. But I don't want to dance if I'm not

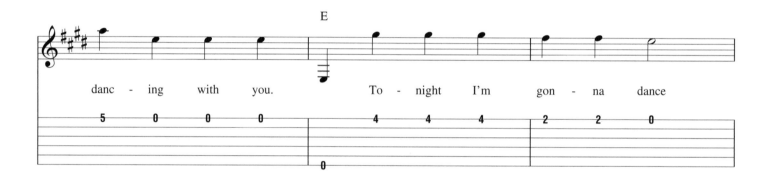

danc - ing with you. To - night I'm gon - na dance

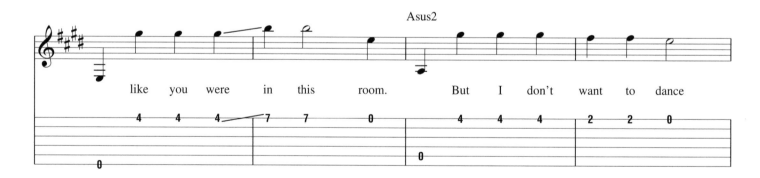

like you were in this room. But I don't want to dance

D.S. al Coda
(take 2nd ending)

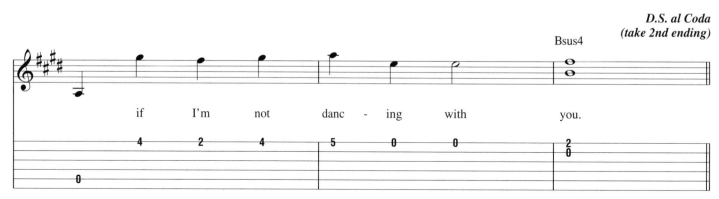

if I'm not danc - ing with you.

$\oplus$ Coda

Outro

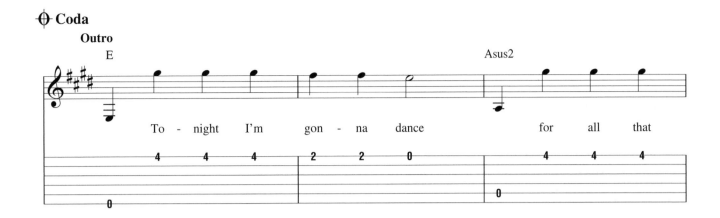

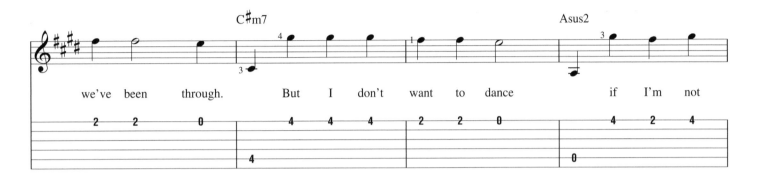

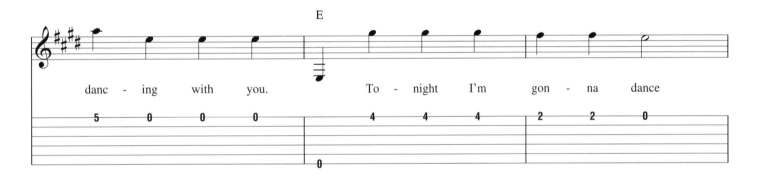

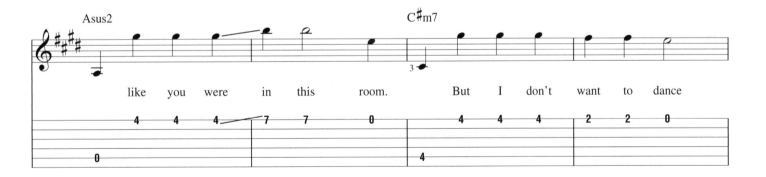

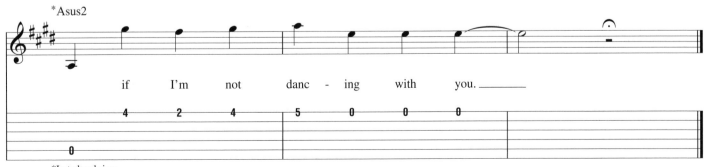

*Let chord ring.

Sad Beautiful Tragic

Words and Music by Taylor Swift

Strum Pattern: 9
Pick Pattern: 7

Intro
Moderately fast

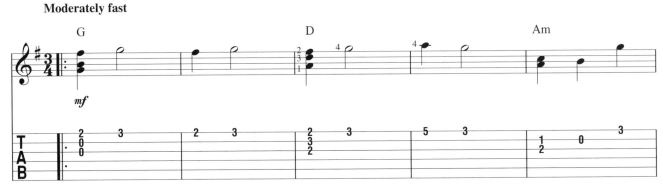

Verse

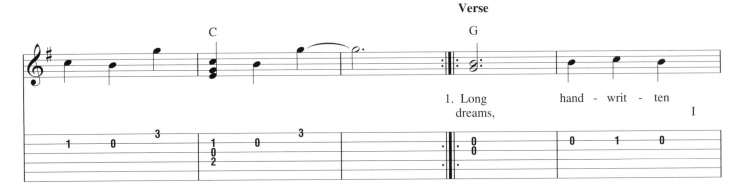

1. Long   hand - writ - ten
   dreams,   I

note   deep   in   your   pock -   et. _____
meet   you   in   warm __   con -   ver - sa -   tion. _____

Words,   how   lit - tle   they   mean __   when you're a   lit - tle   too __
We   both __   wake   in   lone - ly   beds, __   dif - fer - ent

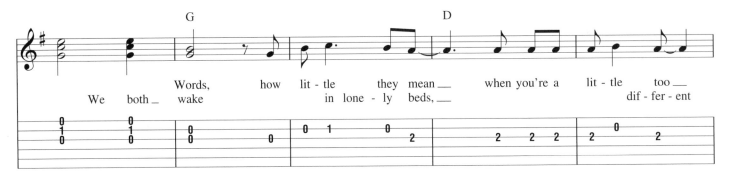

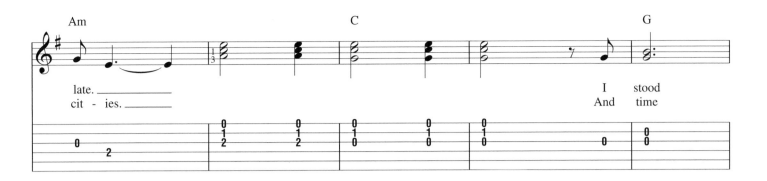

late. _____

cit - ies. _____   I   stood
                                                             And   time

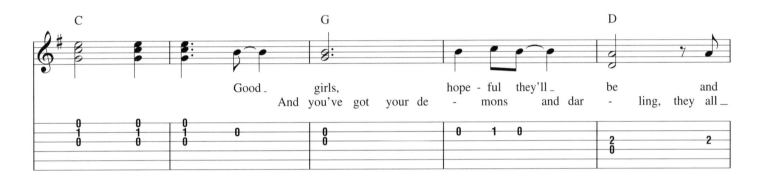

right   by   the   tracks,   your   face   in   a   lock - et. _____
         is   tak - ing   its   sweet ___   time   e - ras - ing   you. ___

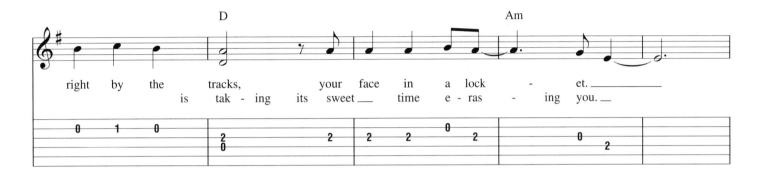

Good ___   girls,   hope - ful   they'll ___   be   and
And   you've   got   your   de - mons   and   dar - ling,   they   all ___

long   will   they _____   wait. _____   We ___
___   look   like   me, _____   'cause   we ___

Chorus

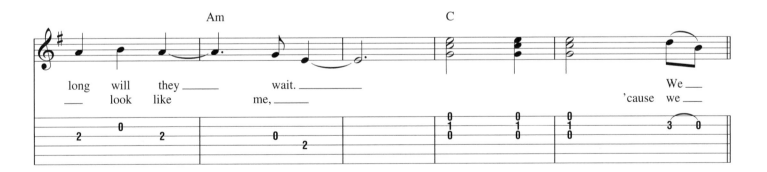

had   a   beau - ti - ful, ___   mag - ic ___   love ___   there. _____

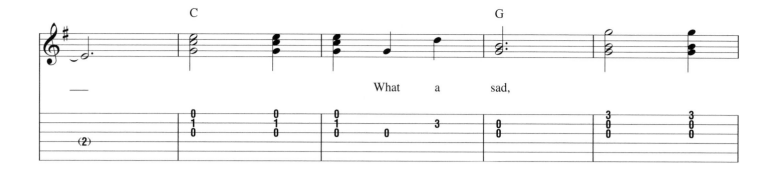

What a sad,

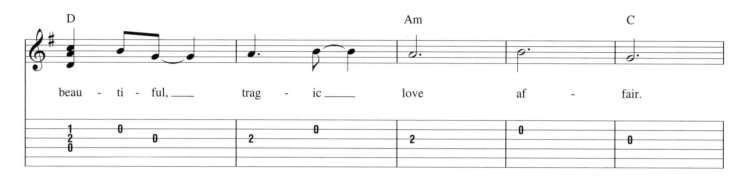

beau - ti - ful, ____ trag - ic ____ love af - fair.

1.

Interlude

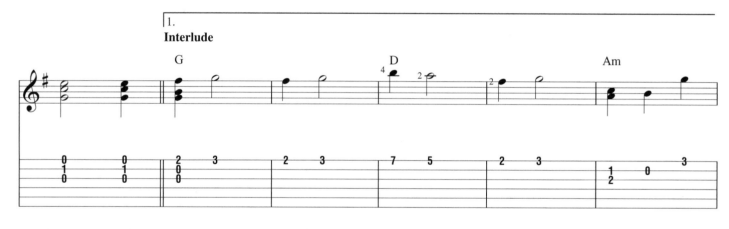

2.

Interlude

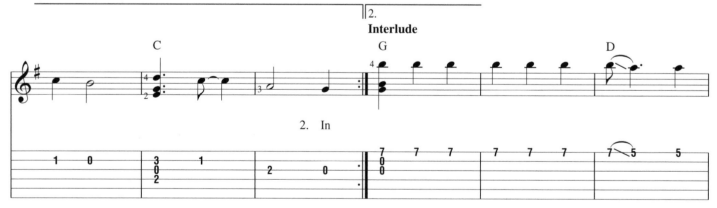

2. In

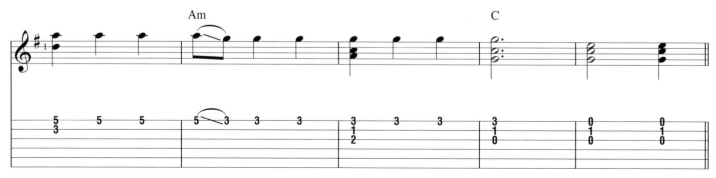

Bridge

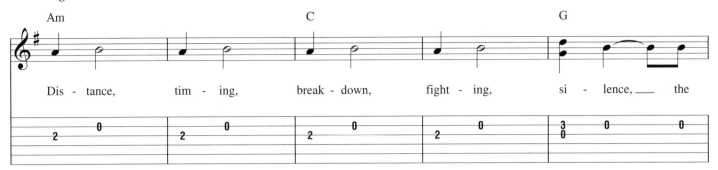

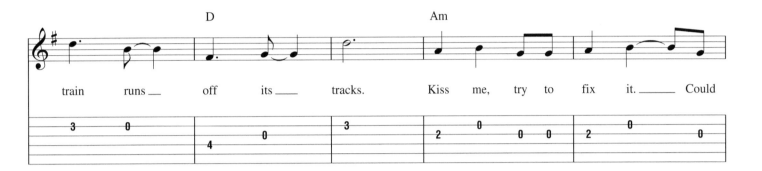

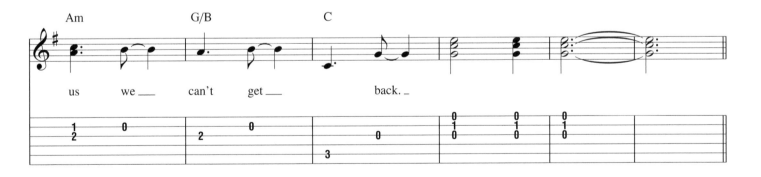

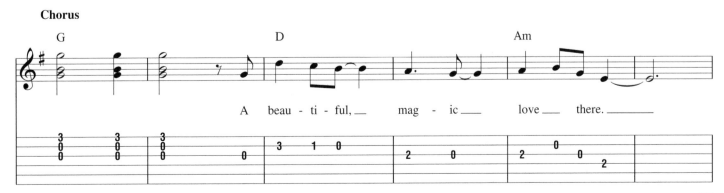

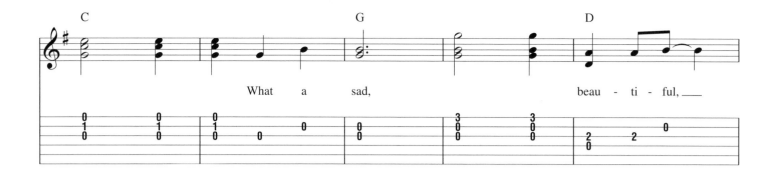

What a sad, beau - ti - ful,___

trag - ic,___ beau - ti - ful, trag - ic,___ beau - ti - ful...___ What we

Outro-Chorus

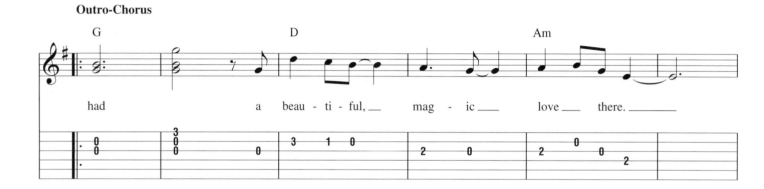

had a beau - ti - ful,___ mag - ic ___ love ___ there.___

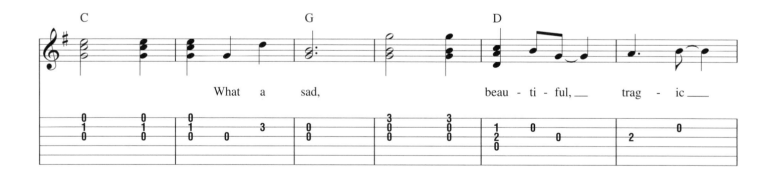

What a sad, beau - ti - ful,___ trag - ic ___

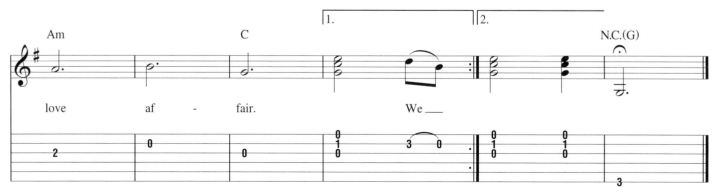

love af - fair. We___

Everything Has Changed

Words and Music by Taylor Swift and Ed Sheeran

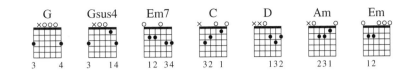

*Tune down 1/2 step:
(low to high) Eb-Ab-Db-Gb-Bb-Eb

Strum Pattern: 6
Pick Pattern: 6

Intro
Moderately slow, in 2

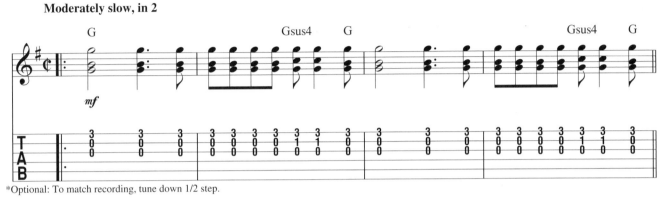

*Optional: To match recording, tune down 1/2 step.

Verse

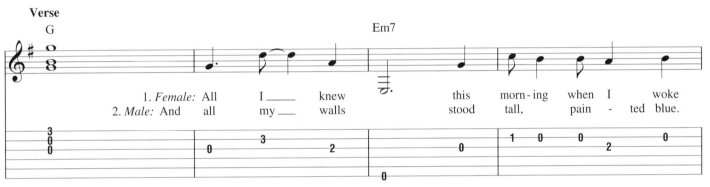

1. *Female:* All I ____ knew this morn-ing when I woke
2. *Male:* And all my ____ walls stood tall, pain-ted blue.

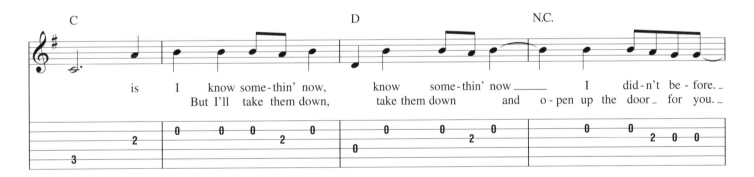

is I know some-thin' now, know some-thin' now ____ I did-n't be-fore. ____
But I'll take them down, take them down and o-pen up the door ____ for you. ____

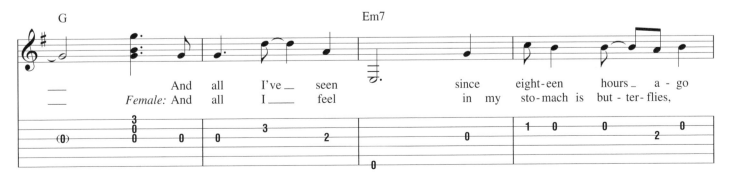

____ And all I've ____ seen since eight-een hours ____ a-go
____ *Female:* And all I ____ feel in my sto-mach is but-ter-flies,

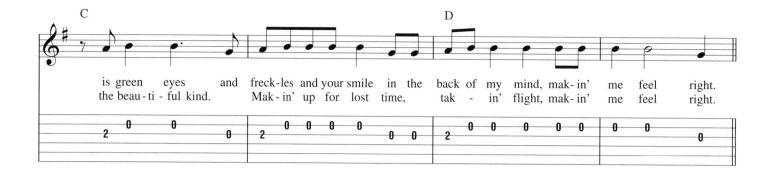

is green eyes and freck-les and your smile in the back of my mind, mak-in' me feel right.
the beau-ti-ful kind. Mak-in' up for lost time, tak - in' flight, mak-in' me feel right.

Pre-Chorus

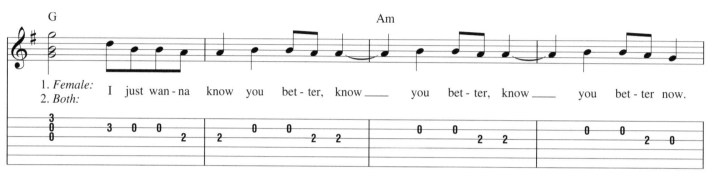

1. *Female:*
2. *Both:* I just wan-na know you bet-ter, know _____ you bet-ter, know _____ you bet-ter now.

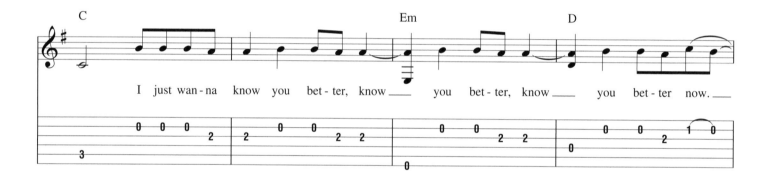

I just wan-na know you bet-ter, know _____ you bet-ter, know _____ you bet-ter now. _____

_____ *Both:* I just wan-na know you bet-ter, know _____ you bet-ter, know _____ you bet-ter now.

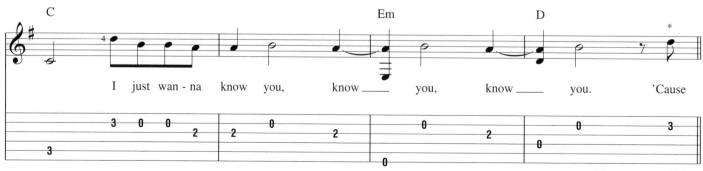

I just wan-na know you, know _____ you, know _____ you. 'Cause

*Sung one octave higher.

% Chorus

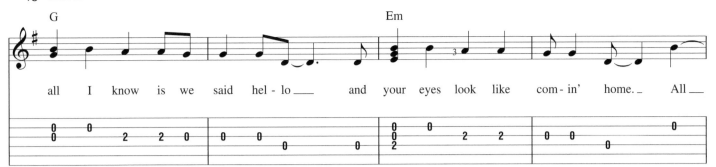

all I know is we said hel - lo ___ and your eyes look like com - in' home. _ All __

__ I know is a sim - ple name. ___ Ev - 'ry - thing ___ has changed.

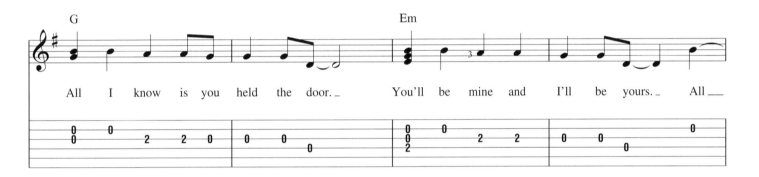

All I know is you held the door. _ You'll be mine and I'll be yours. _ All __

To Coda ⊕

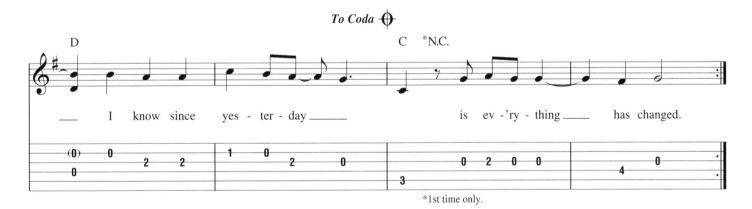

__ I know since yes - ter - day ___ is ev - 'ry - thing ___ has changed.

*1st time only.

Bridge

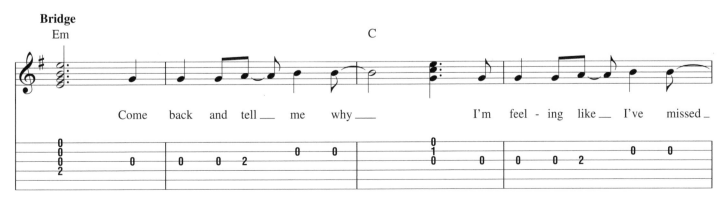

Come back and tell __ me why ___ I'm feel - ing like __ I've missed _

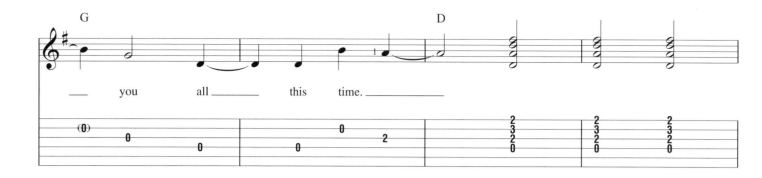

you all _____ this time. _____

And meet me there __ to - night. ___ And let me know __ that it's _

__ not all _____ in my ____ mind. _____

Pre-Chorus

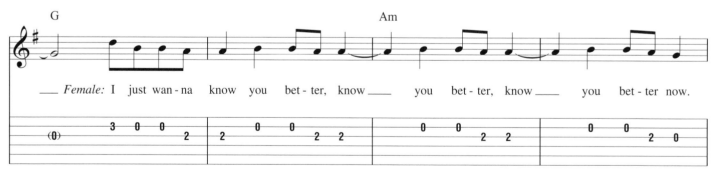

__ *Female:* I just wan - na know you bet - ter, know ____ you bet - ter, know ____ you bet - ter now.

D.S. al Coda

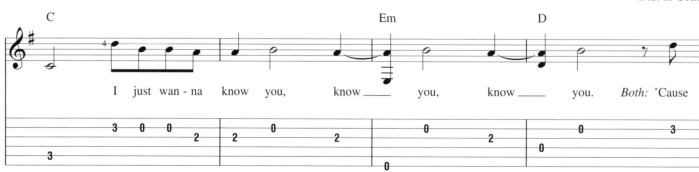

I just wan - na know you, know ____ you, know ____ you. *Both:* 'Cause

70

The Lucky One

Words and Music by Taylor Swift

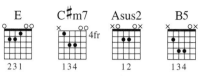

Strum Pattern: 1
Pick Pattern: 4

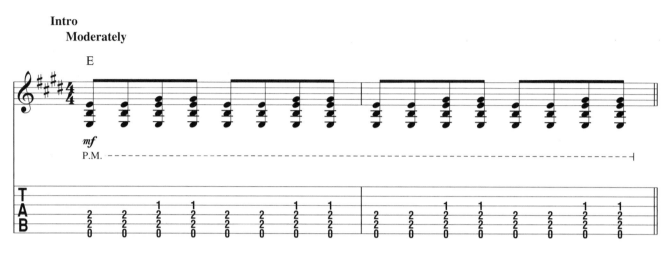

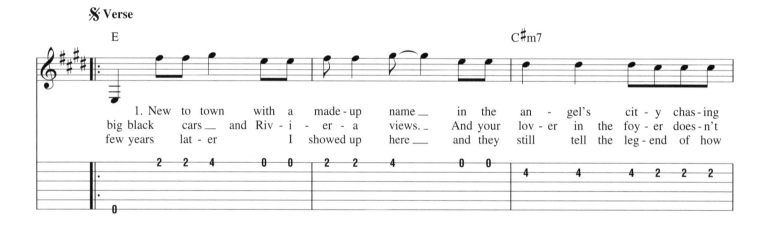

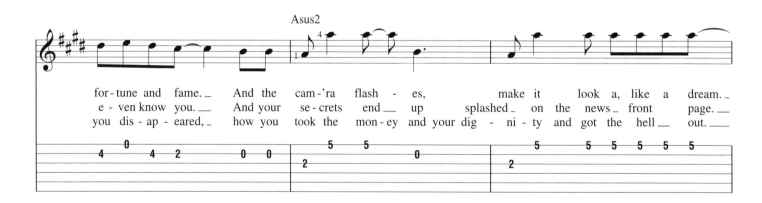

1. New to town with a made-up name in the an - gel's cit - y chas - ing
big black cars and Riv - i - er - a views. And your lov - er in the foy - er does - n't
few years lat - er I showed up here and they still tell the leg - end of how

for - tune and fame. And the cam - 'ra flash - es, make it look a, like a dream.
e - ven know you. And your se - crets end up splashed on the news front page.
you dis - ap - eared, how you took the mon - ey and your dig - ni - ty and got the hell out.

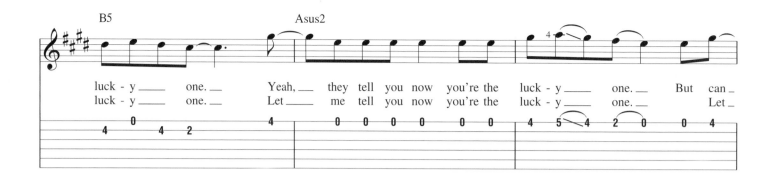

luck - y _____ one. _____ Yeah, _____ they tell you now you're the luck - y _____ one. _____ But can _
luck - y _____ one. _____ Let _____ me tell you now you're the luck - y _____ one. _____ Let _

To Coda ⊕

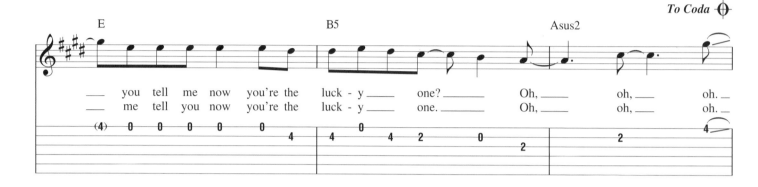

_____ you tell me now you're the luck - y _____ one? _____ Oh, _____ oh, _____ oh. _
_____ me tell you now you're the luck - y _____ one. _____ Oh, _____ oh, _____ oh. _

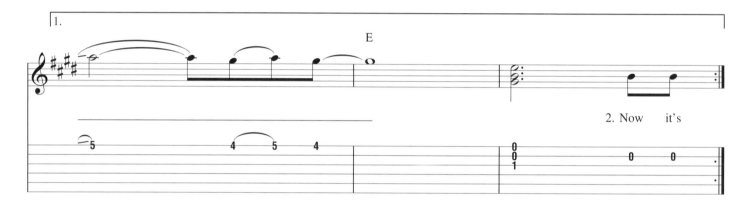

2. Now it's

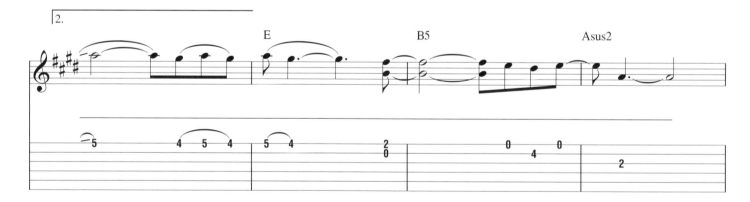

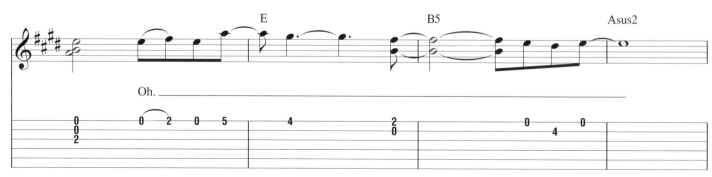

Oh. _____

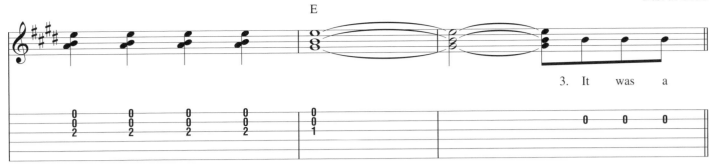

Coda

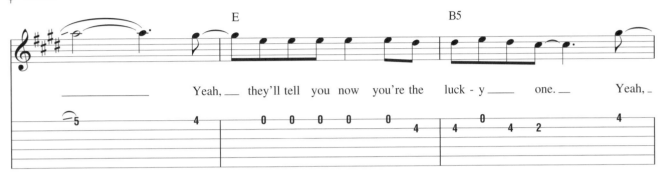

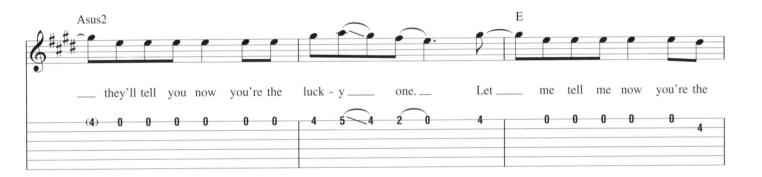

Starlight

Words and Music by Taylor Swift

Strum Pattern: 1
Pick Pattern: 2

Chorus
Moderately

I said oh my, what a mar-vel-ous tune.__ It was the best night, nev-er would for-

*Chord symbols reflect overall harmony.

get how he moved.__ The whole place_____ was dressed to the nines__ and we were

danc-ing, danc-ing_____ like__ we're made of star - light,

like__ we're made of star - light.

Verse

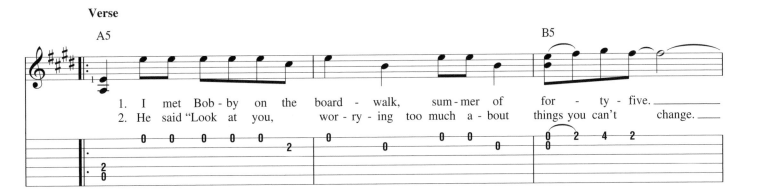

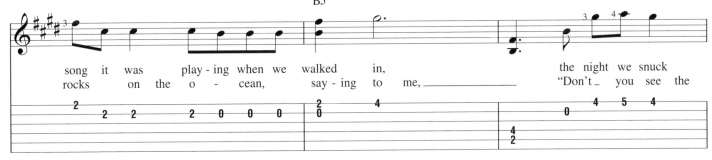

%: **Chorus**

And I said oh
Like oh my, what a mar-vel-ous tune. __ It was the
Oh

best night, nev-er would for-get how he moved. __ The whole place ___ was

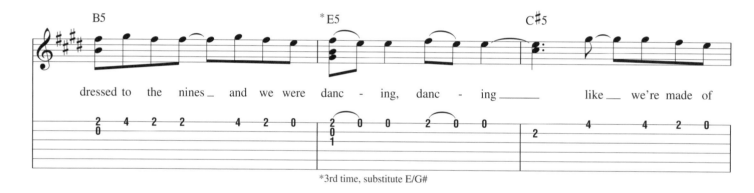

dressed to the nines __ and we were danc-ing, danc-ing ___ like __ we're made of

*3rd time, substitute E/G#

To Coda ⊕

star-light, star-light, like __ we're made of star-light, star-light. ___

2.

Bridge

Ooh, _____ ooh, _____ he's _____ talk-in' _____ cra - zy, ooh, _____ ooh, _____ danc -

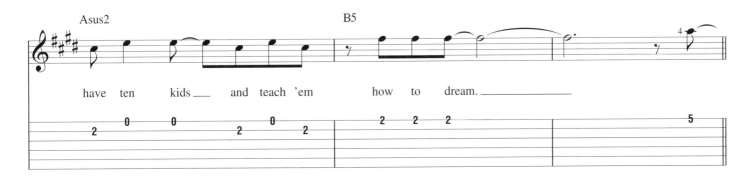

- in' with me. Ooh, _____ ooh, _____ we _____ could get a, mar - ried,

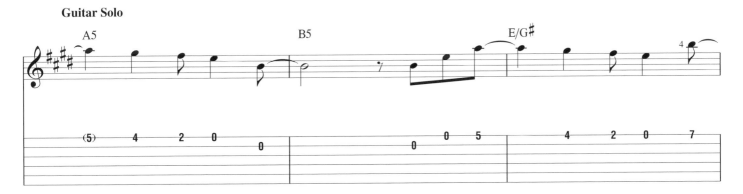

have ten kids _____ and teach 'em how to dream. _____

Guitar Solo

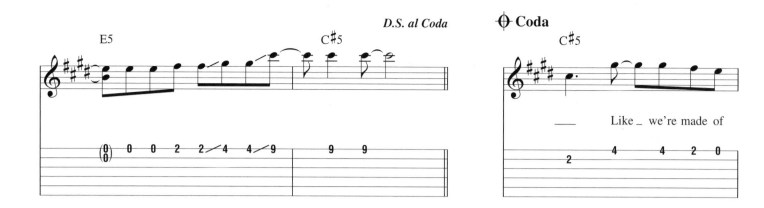

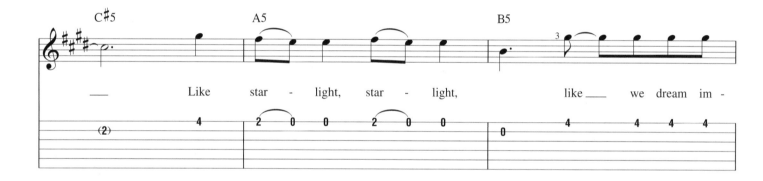

Begin Again

Words and Music by Taylor Swift

Strum Pattern: 2
Pick Pattern: 4

Intro
Moderately slow, in 2

(G5)

Verse

(G5)

1. Took a deep breath in the mir - ror.
2. Walked in ex - pect - ing you'd be late, but you
3. You said you nev - er met one girl who had as

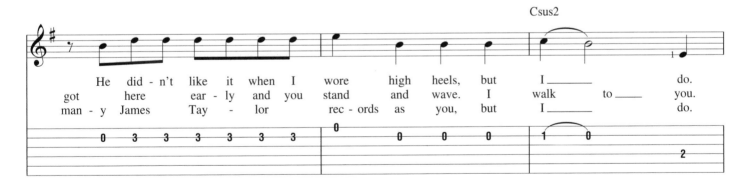

He did - n't like it when I wore high heels, but I_____ do.
got here ear - ly and you stand and wave. I walk to_____ you.
man - y James Tay - lor rec - ords as you, but I_____ do.

(Csus2)

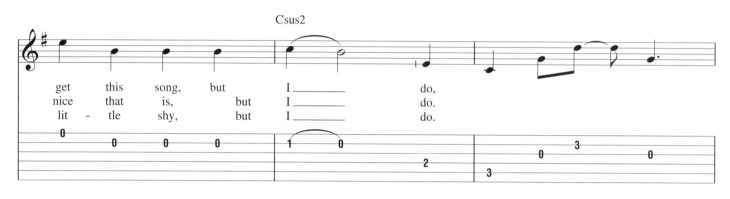

𝄉 Chorus

he nev-er did. _____ And I've been spend-ing the last __

__ eight months think-ing all __ love ev-er does __ is

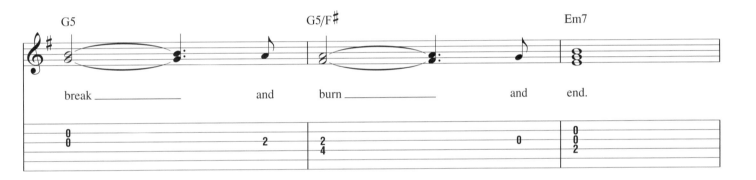

break _____ and burn _____ and end.

But on a Wednes-day in a ca-fe

To Coda 1 ⊕
To Coda 2 ⊕

D.C. al Coda 1
(take 2nd ending)

I watched __ it be-gin a-gain.

⊕ **Coda 1**

__ it be-gin a-gain.

Interlude

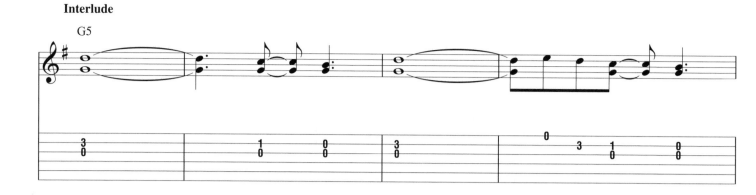

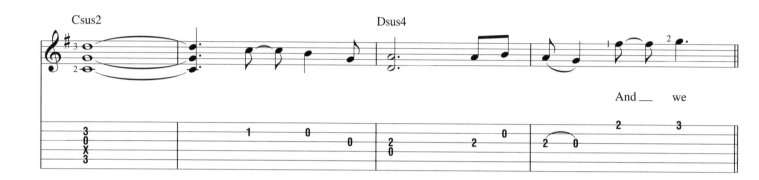

And __ we

Bridge

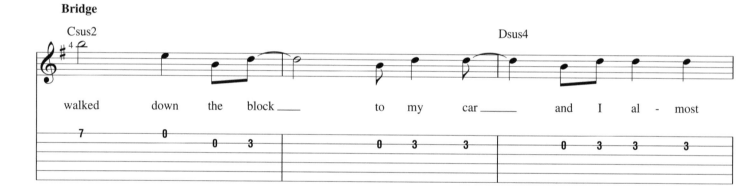

walked   down   the   block ___   to   my   car ___   and   I   al - most

brought   him   up,   but   you   start   to   talk ___   a - bout   the   mov -

- ies   that   your   fam - 'ly   watch - es   ev - 'ry   sin - gle   Christ-

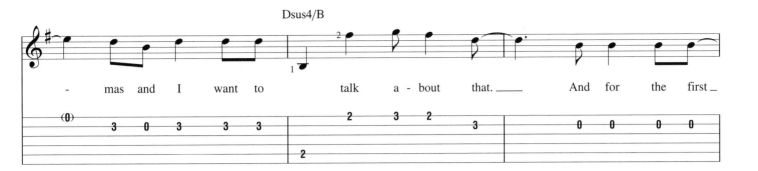

-mas and I want to talk a-bout that. _____ And for the first _

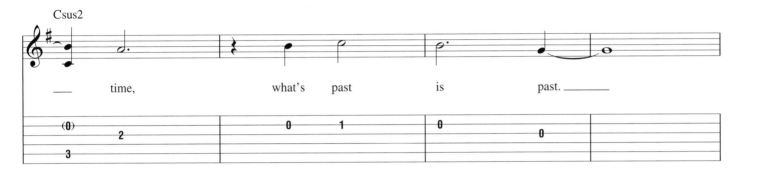

_ time, what's past is past. _____

 D.S. al Coda 2
(take 2nd ending)

⊕ Coda 2

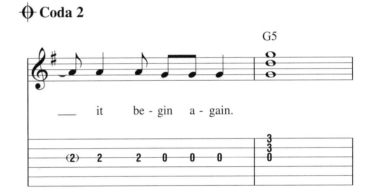

_ it be-gin a-gain.

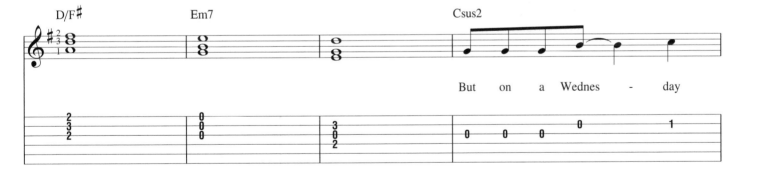

But on a Wednes - day

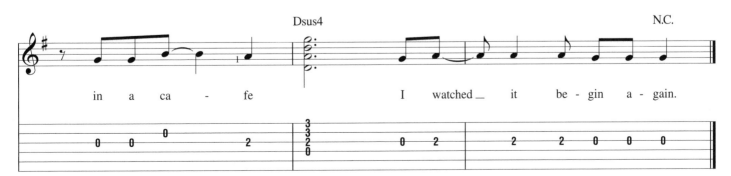

in a ca - fe   I watched _ it be-gin a-gain.

EASY GUITAR WITH NOTES & TAB

This series features simplified arrangements with notes, tab, chord charts, and strum and pick patterns.

MIXED FOLIOS

00702287 Acoustic $14.99	00702257 Easy Acoustic Guitar Songs $14.99	00702271 1960s Rock $14.99
00702002 Acoustic Rock Hits for Easy Guitar $12.95	00702280 Easy Guitar Tab White Pages $29.99	00702270 1970s Rock $14.99
00702166 All-Time Best Guitar Collection........... $19.99	00702212 Essential Christmas $9.95	00702269 1980s Rock $14.99
00699665 Beatles Best $12.95	00702041 Favorite Hymns for Easy Guitar $9.95	00702268 1990s Rock $14.99
00702232 Best Acoustic Songs for Easy Guitar.... $12.99	00702281 4 Chord Rock $9.99	00702187 Selections from
00702233 Best Hard Rock Songs $14.99	00702286 Glee $16.99	O Brother Where Art Thou?............. $12.95
00703055 The Big Book of Nursery Rhymes	00702174 God Bless America®	00702178 100 Songs for Kids $12.95
& Children's Songs $14.99	& Other Songs for a Better Nation....... $8.95	00702515 Pirates of the Caribbean $12.99
00698978 Big Christmas Collection $16.95	00699374 Gospel Favorites $14.95	00702125 Praise and Worship for Guitar $9.95
00702394 Bluegrass Songs for Easy Guitar $12.99	00702160 The Great American Country	00702155 Rock Hits for Guitar $9.95
00702149 Children's Christian Songbook $7.95	Songbook.. $15.99	00702110 The Sound of Music $9.99
00702237 Christian Acoustic Favorites............... $12.95	00702050 Great Classical Themes for Easy Guitar $6.95	00702285 Southern Rock Hits $12.99
00702028 Christmas Classics $7.95	00702131 Great Country Hits of the '90s $8.95	00702866 Theme Music $12.99
00702185 Christmas Hits.................................. $9.95	00702116 Greatest Hymns for Guitar $8.95	00702124 Today's Christian Rock – 2nd Edition . $9.95
00702016 Classic Blues for Easy Guitar $12.95	00702130 The Groovy Years $9.95	00702220 Today's Country Hits......................... $9.95
00702141 Classic Rock...................................... $8.95	00702184 Guitar Instrumentals $9.95	00702198 Today's Hits for Guitar $9.95
00702203 CMT's 100 Greatest Country Songs $27.95	00702046 Hits of the '70s for Easy Guitar............. $8.95	00702217 Top Christian Hits $12.95
00702283 The Contemporary Christian	00702273 Irish Songs $12.99	00702235 Top Christian Hits of '07-'08 .... $14.95
Collection $16.99	00702275 Jazz Favorites for Easy Guitar $14.99	00702556 Top Hits of 2011 .... $14.99
00702006 Contemporary Christian Favorites......... $9.95	00702274 Jazz Standards for Easy Guitar $14.99	00702294 Top Worship Hits $14.99
00702239 Country Classics for Easy Guitar $19.99	00702162 Jumbo Easy Guitar Songbook............ $19.95	00702206 Very Best of Rock............................. $9.95
00702282 Country Hits of 2009-2010 .... $14.99	00702258 Legends of Rock $14.99	00702255 VH1's 100 Greatest Hard Rock Songs .. $27.95
00702240 Country Hits of 2007-2008 .... $12.95	00702261 Modern Worship Hits $14.99	00702175 VH1's 100 Greatest Songs of
00702225 Country Hits of '06-'07...................... $12.95	00702189 MTV's 100 Greatest Pop Songs $24.95	Rock and Roll................................. $24.95
00702085 Disney Movie Hits.............................. $12.95	00702272 1950s Rock $14.99	00702253 Wicked $12.99

ARTIST COLLECTIONS

00702267 AC/DC for Easy Guitar $15.99	00702099 Best of Amy Grant $9.95	00702139 Elvis Country Favorites $9.95
00702598 Adele for Easy Guitar $14.99	00702190 Best of Pat Green $19.95	00702293 The Very Best of Prince $12.99
00702001 Best of Aerosmith.............................. $16.95	00702136 Best of Merle Haggard $12.99	00699415 Best of Queen for Guitar $14.99
00702040 Best of the Allman Brothers $14.99	00702243 Hannah Montana $14.95	00702208 Red Hot Chili Peppers – Greatest Hits $12.95
00702865 J.S. Bach for Easy Guitar $12.99	00702244 Hannah Montana 2/Meet Miley Cyrus... $16.95	00702093 Rolling Stones Collection.................... $17.95
00702169 Best of The Beach Boys...................... $12.99	00702227 Jimi Hendrix – Smash Hits................. $14.99	00702092 Best of the Rolling Stones.................. $14.99
00702292 The Beatles – 1 .... $19.99	00702288 Best of Hillsong United $12.99	00702196 Best of Bob Seger............................ $12.95
00702201 The Essential Black Sabbath............... $12.95	00702236 Best of Antonio Carlos Jobim $12.95	00702252 Frank Sinatra – Nothing But the Best $12.99
00702140 Best of Brooks & Dunn $10.95	00702245 Elton John –	00702010 Best of Rod Stewart $14.95
02501615 Zac Brown Band – The Foundation .. $16.99	Greatest Hits 1970-2002 .... $14.99	00702049 Best of George Strait $12.95
02501621 Zac Brown Band –	00702204 Robert Johnson................................ $9.95	00702259 Taylor Swift for Easy Guitar $14.99
You Get What You Give $16.99	00702277 Best of Jonas Brothers $14.99	00702290 Taylor Swift – Speak Now $14.99
00702095 Best of Mariah Carey.......................... $12.95	00702234 Selections from Toby Keith –	00702223 Chris Tomlin – Arriving...................... $12.95
00702043 Best of Johnny Cash.......................... $16.99	35 Biggest Hits $12.95	00702262 Chris Tomlin Collection...................... $14.99
00702033 Best of Steven Curtis Chapman........... $14.95	00702003 Kiss $9.95	00702226 Chris Tomlin – See the Morning........ $12.95
00702291 Very Best of Coldplay $12.99	00702193 Best of Jennifer Knapp $12.95	00702132 Shania Twain – Greatest Hits.............. $10.95
00702263 Best of Casting Crowns $12.99	00702097 John Lennon – Imagine $9.95	00702427 U2 – 18 Singles $14.99
00702090 Eric Clapton's Best $10.95	00702216 Lynyrd Skynyrd................................ $15.99	00702108 Best of Stevie Ray Vaughan $10.95
00702086 Eric Clapton –	00702182 The Essential Bob Marley.................. $12.95	00702123 Best of Hank Williams....................... $12.99
from the Album Unplugged $10.95	00702346 Bruno Mars –	00702111 Stevie Wonder – Guitar Collection........ $9.95
00702202 The Essential Eric Clapton................. $12.95	Doo-Wops & Hooligans $12.99	00702228 Neil Young – Greatest Hits $15.99
00702250 blink-182 – Greatest Hits $12.99	00702248 Paul McCartney – All the Best $14.99	00702188 Essential ZZ Top............................... $10.95
00702053 Best of Patsy Cline............................ $10.95	00702129 Songs of Sarah McLachlan $12.95	
00702229 The Very Best of	02501316 Metallica – Death Magnetic $15.95	*Prices, contents and availability*
Creedence Clearwater Revival............. $14.99	00702209 Steve Miller Band –	*subject to change without notice.*
00702145 Best of Jim Croce.............................. $12.99	Young Hearts (Greatest Hits) $12.95	
00702278 Crosby, Stills & Nash $12.99	00702096 Best of Nirvana................................ $14.95	
00702219 David Crowder*Band Collection........ $12.95	00702211 The Offspring – Greatest Hits............. $12.95	
00702122 The Doors for Easy Guitar.................. $12.99	00702030 Best of Roy Orbison $12.95	
00702276 Fleetwood Mac –	00702144 Best of Ozzy Osbourne $14.99	
Easy Guitar Collection $12.99	00702279 Tom Petty $12.99	

HAL•LEONARD® CORPORATION

7777 W. BLUEMOUND RD. P.O. BOX 13819 MILWAUKEE, WI 53213

Visit Hal Leonard online at
www.halleonard.com

0712

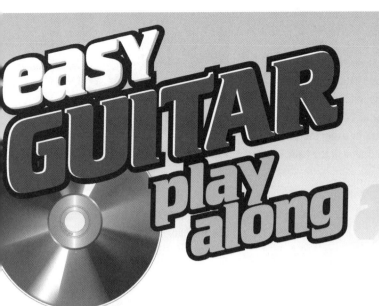

easy GUITAR play along

1. ROCK CLASSICS

INCLUDES TAB

Jailbreak • Living After Midnight • Mississippi Queen • Rocks Off • Runnin' Down a Dream • Smoke on the Water • Strutter • Up Around the Bend.

00702560 Book/CD Pack..$14.99

4. ROCK 'N' ROLL

INCLUDES TAB

Blue Suede Shoes • I Get Around • I'm a Believer • Jailhouse Rock • Oh, Pretty Woman • Peggy Sue • Runaway • Wake up Little Susie.

00702572 Book/CD Pack..$14.99

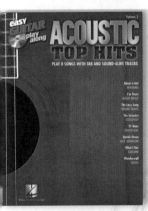

2. ACOUSTIC TOP HITS

INCLUDES TAB

About a Girl • I'm Yours • The Lazy Song • The Scientist • 21 Guns • Upside Down • What I Got • Wonderwall.

00702569 Book/CD Pack..$14.99

5. ULTIMATE ACOUSTIC

INCLUDES TAB

Against the Wind • Babe, I'm Gonna Leave You • Come Monday • Free Fallin' • Give a Little Bit • Have You Ever Seen the Rain? • New Kid in Town • We Can Work It Out.

00702573 Book/CD Pack..$14.99

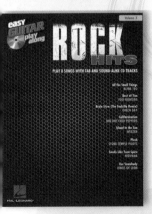

3. ROCK HITS

INCLUDES TAB

All the Small Things • Best of You • Brain Stew (The Godzilla Remix) • Californication • Island in the Sun • Plush • Smells like Teen Spirit • Use Somebody.

00702570 Book/CD Pack..$14.99

6. CHRISTMAS SONGS

INCLUDES TAB

Have Yourself a Merry Little Christmas • A Holly Jolly Christmas • The Little Drummer Boy • Run Rudolph Run • Santa Claus Is Comin' to Town • Silver and Gold • Sleigh Ride • Winter Wonderland.

00101879 Book/CD Pack...................................$14.99

HAL•LEONARD® CORPORATION

7777 W. BLUEMOUND RD. P.O. BOX 13819
MILWAUKEE, WISCONSIN 53213

www.halleonard.com

0712

HAL•LEONARD GUITAR PLAY•ALONG

This series will help you play your favorite songs quickly and easily. Just follow the tab and listen to the CD to the hear how the guitar should sound, and then play along using the separate backing tracks. Mac or PC users can also slow down the tempo without changing pitch by using the CD in their computer. The melody and lyrics are included in the book so that you can sing or simply follow along.

INCLUDES TAB

VOL. 1 – ROCK	00699570 / $16.99
VOL. 2 – ACOUSTIC	00699569 / $16.95
VOL. 3 – HARD ROCK	00699573 / $16.95
VOL. 4 – POP/ROCK	00699571 / $16.99
VOL. 5 – MODERN ROCK	00699574 / $16.99
VOL. 6 – '90s ROCK	00699572 / $16.99
VOL. 7 – BLUES	00699575 / $16.95
VOL. 8 – ROCK	00699585 / $14.99
VOL. 9 – PUNK ROCK	00699576 / $14.95
VOL. 10 – ACOUSTIC	00699586 / $16.95
VOL. 11 – EARLY ROCK	00699579 / $14.95
VOL. 12 – POP/ROCK	00699587 / $14.95
VOL. 13 – FOLK ROCK	00699581 / $15.99
VOL. 14 – BLUES ROCK	00699582 / $16.95
VOL. 15 – R&B	00699583 / $14.95
VOL. 16 – JAZZ	00699584 / $15.95
VOL. 17 – COUNTRY	00699588 / $15.95
VOL. 18 – ACOUSTIC ROCK	00699577 / $15.95
VOL. 19 – SOUL	00699578 / $14.99
VOL. 20 – ROCKABILLY	00699580 / $14.95
VOL. 21 – YULETIDE	00699602 / $14.95
VOL. 22 – CHRISTMAS	00699600 / $15.95
VOL. 23 – SURF	00699635 / $14.95
VOL. 24 – ERIC CLAPTON	00699649 / $17.99
VOL. 25 – LENNON & McCARTNEY	00699642 / $16.99
VOL. 26 – ELVIS PRESLEY	00699643 / $14.95
VOL. 27 – DAVID LEE ROTH	00699645 / $16.95
VOL. 28 – GREG KOCH	00699646 / $14.95
VOL. 29 – BOB SEGER	00699647 / $15.99
VOL. 30 – KISS	00699644 / $16.99
VOL. 31 – CHRISTMAS HITS	00699652 / $14.95
VOL. 32 – THE OFFSPRING	00699653 / $14.95
VOL. 33 – ACOUSTIC CLASSICS	00699656 / $16.95
VOL. 34 – CLASSIC ROCK	00699658 / $16.95
VOL. 35 – HAIR METAL	00699660 / $16.95
VOL. 36 – SOUTHERN ROCK	00699661 / $16.95
VOL. 37 – ACOUSTIC METAL	00699662 / $16.95
VOL. 38 – BLUES	00699663 / $16.95
VOL. 39 – '80s METAL	00699664 / $16.99
VOL. 40 – INCUBUS	00699668 / $17.95
VOL. 41 – ERIC CLAPTON	00699669 / $16.95
VOL. 42 – 2000s ROCK	00699670 / $16.99
VOL. 43 – LYNYRD SKYNYRD	00699681 / $17.95
VOL. 44 – JAZZ	00699689 / $14.99
VOL. 45 – TV THEMES	00699718 / $14.95
VOL. 46 – MAINSTREAM ROCK	00699722 / $16.95
VOL. 47 – HENDRIX SMASH HITS	00699723 / $19.95
VOL. 48 – AEROSMITH CLASSICS	00699724 / $17.99
VOL. 49 – STEVIE RAY VAUGHAN	00699725 / $17.99
VOL. 51 – ALTERNATIVE '90s	00699727 / $14.95

VOL. 52 – FUNK	00699728 / $14.95
VOL. 53 – DISCO	00699729 / $14.99
VOL. 54 – HEAVY METAL	00699730 / $14.95
VOL. 55 – POP METAL	00699731 / $14.95
VOL. 56 – FOO FIGHTERS	00699749 / $15.99
VOL. 57 – SYSTEM OF A DOWN	00699751 / $14.95
VOL. 58 – BLINK-182	00699772 / $14.95
VOL. 60 – 3 DOORS DOWN	00699774 / $14.95
VOL. 61 – SLIPKNOT	00699775 / $16.99
VOL. 62 – CHRISTMAS CAROLS	00699798 / $12.95
VOL. 63 – CREEDENCE CLEARWATER REVIVAL	00699802 / $16.99
VOL. 64 – THE ULTIMATE OZZY OSBOURNE	00699803 / $16.99
VOL. 65 – THE DOORS	00699806 / $16.99
VOL. 66 – THE ROLLING STONES	00699807 / $16.95
VOL. 67 – BLACK SABBATH	00699808 / $16.99
VOL. 68 – PINK FLOYD – DARK SIDE OF THE MOON	00699809 / $16.99
VOL. 69 – ACOUSTIC FAVORITES	00699810 / $14.95
VOL. 70 – OZZY OSBOURNE	00699805 / $16.99
VOL. 71 – CHRISTIAN ROCK	00699824 / $14.95
VOL. 72 – ACOUSTIC '90s	00699827 / $14.95
VOL. 73 – BLUESY ROCK	00699829 / $16.99
VOL. 74 – PAUL BALOCHE	00699831 / $14.95
VOL. 75 – TOM PETTY	00699882 / $16.99
VOL. 76 – COUNTRY HITS	00699884 / $14.95
VOL. 77 – BLUEGRASS	00699910 / $14.99
VOL. 78 – NIRVANA	00700132 / $16.99
VOL. 79 – NEIL YOUNG	00700133 / $24.99
VOL. 80 – ACOUSTIC ANTHOLOGY	00700175 / $19.95
VOL. 81 – ROCK ANTHOLOGY	00700176 / $22.99
VOL. 82 – EASY SONGS	00700177 / $12.99
VOL. 83 – THREE CHORD SONGS	00700178 / $16.99
VOL. 84 – STEELY DAN	00700200 / $16.99
VOL. 85 – THE POLICE	00700269 / $16.99
VOL. 86 – BOSTON	00700465 / $16.99
VOL. 87 – ACOUSTIC WOMEN	00700763 / $14.99
VOL. 88 – GRUNGE	00700467 / $16.99
VOL. 90 – CLASSICAL POP	00700469 / $14.99
VOL. 91 – BLUES INSTRUMENTALS	00700505 / $14.99
VOL. 92 – EARLY ROCK INSTRUMENTALS	00700506 / $14.99
VOL. 93 – ROCK INSTRUMENTALS	00700507 / $16.99
VOL. 95 – BLUES CLASSICS	00700509 / $14.99
VOL. 96 – THIRD DAY	00700560 / $14.95
VOL. 97 – ROCK BAND	00700703 / $14.99
VOL. 98 – ROCK BAND	00700704 / $14.95
VOL. 99 – ZZ TOP	00700762 / $16.99
VOL. 100 – B.B. KING	00700466 / $16.99
VOL. 101 – SONGS FOR BEGINNERS	00701917 / $14.99
VOL. 102 – CLASSIC PUNK	00700769 / $14.99

VOL. 103 – SWITCHFOOT	00700773 / $16.99
VOL. 104 – DUANE ALLMAN	00700846 / $16.99
VOL. 106 – WEEZER	00700958 / $14.99
VOL. 107 – CREAM	00701069 / $16.99
VOL. 108 – THE WHO	00701053 / $16.99
VOL. 109 – STEVE MILLER	00701054 / $14.99
VOL. 111 – JOHN MELLENCAMP	00701056 / $14.99
VOL. 112 – QUEEN	00701052 / $16.99
VOL. 113 – JIM CROCE	00701058 / $15.99
VOL. 114 – BON JOVI	00701060 / $14.99
VOL. 115 – JOHNNY CASH	00701070 / $16.99
VOL. 116 – THE VENTURES	00701124 / $14.99
VOL. 118 – ERIC JOHNSON	00701353 / $14.99
VOL. 119 – AC/DC CLASSICS	00701356 / $17.99
VOL. 120 – PROGRESSIVE ROCK	00701457 / $14.99
VOL. 121 – U2	00701508 / $16.99
VOL. 123 – LENNON & MCCARTNEY ACOUSTIC	00701614 / $16.99
VOL. 124 – MODERN WORSHIP	00701629 / $14.99
VOL. 125 – JEFF BECK	00701687 / $16.99
VOL. 126 – BOB MARLEY	00701701 / $16.99
VOL. 127 – 1970s ROCK	00701739 / $14.99
VOL. 128 – 1960s ROCK	00701740 / $14.99
VOL. 129 – MEGADETH	00701741 / $16.99
VOL. 131 – 1990s ROCK	00701743 / $14.99
VOL. 132 – COUNTRY ROCK	00701757 / $15.99
VOL. 133 – TAYLOR SWIFT	00701894 / $16.99
VOL. 134 – AVENGED SEVENFOLD	00701906 / $16.99
VOL. 136 – GUITAR THEMES	00701922 / $14.99
VOL. 138 – BLUEGRASS CLASSICS	00701967 / $14.99
VOL. 139 – GARY MOORE	00702370 / $16.99
VOL. 140 – MORE STEVIE RAY VAUGHAN	00702396 / $17.99
VOL. 141 – ACOUSTIC HITS	00702401 / $16.99
VOL. 142 – KINGS OF LEON	00702418 / $16.99
VOL. 145 – DEF LEPPARD	00702532 / $16.99
VOL. 147 – SIMON & GARFUNKEL	14041591 / $16.99
VOL. 149 – AC/DC HITS	14041593 / $17.99
VOL. 150 – ZAKK WYLDE	02501717 / $16.99
VOL. 153 – RED HOT CHILI PEPPERS	00702990 / $19.99
VOL. 166 – MODERN BLUES	00700764 / $16.99

Complete song lists available online.

Prices, contents, and availability subject to change without notice.

HAL•LEONARD® CORPORATION

7777 W. BLUEMOUND RD. P.O. BOX 13819 MILWAUKEE, WI 53213

Visit Hal Leonard online at
www.halleonard.com

0812